"I've known and trusted Barrett Johnson for many years, and I'm thrilled that he has written this book. The mindset of discipling our children to look like and follow Jesus can so easily get lost in the usual parenting resources. Every child will need to make the choice to follow Jesus for themselves. But this book will, as Barrett puts it, help you to do what *you* can to make the choice a no-brainer."

> Shaunti Feldhahn, social researcher, speaker, bestselling
> author of several books, including *For Women Only*
> and *For Parents Only*

"Jesus had an intentional plan to disciple His disciples. In Christ's example, we find a powerful model for parents who want to help their children follow Him as well. The Scripture in this book will strengthen your faith and your family and help you grow as a parent."

> Dr. Rob Rienow, founder of Visionary Family Ministries

"Barrett Johnson equips readers (both parents and grand-parents alike) to drop back and think intentionally. He stirs me to ask myself, *How am I modeling, teaching, and applying biblical truth in my kids' (and grands') lives as a discipling parent?* Read this book, take it to heart and action, pass it to others, and rest assured that Barrett is a trustworthy guide in the journey of parenting."

> Dr. Gary Rosberg, cofounder of America's Family Coaches

"Parents want to launch kids into adulthood with lives marked by character, depth, and purpose. Foundational to achieving that is helping our children learn to love and follow Jesus.

Barrett Johnson's easy-to-read book gives a biblical framework that guides parents in doing exactly that."

John Rosemond, author of *The Bible Parenting Code*,
public speaker, podcaster

"Christian parents regularly hear the challenge to disciple their children. Many know they should. But most do not know how to start. This book is the way forward. Barrett Johnson provides a helpful blend of practical and biblical wisdom so that parents can be intentional about discipling their kids in the ways of Jesus."

Pastor Clay Smith, senior pastor, Johnson Ferry Baptist
Church, Marietta, Georgia

"Raising children today is hard work. Guiding them to be disciples of Christ is even more challenging. This book will not only tell you what to do but how to do it."

Dr. Scott Turansky, cofounder of the National Center
for Biblical Parenting

DISCIPLE
THEM LIKE
Jesus

RESOURCES BY BARRETT AND JENIFER JOHNSON

The Talk(s): A Parent's Guide to Critical Conversations about Sex, Dating, and Other Unmentionables

The Young Man's Guide to Awesomeness: How to Guard Your Heart, Get the Girl and Save the World

Meet Me in the Middle: 10 Conversations for Dads and Daughters

Smartphones 101 Online Course: Smartphones-101.com

The Talk(s) Video Series

DISCIPLE THEM LIKE *Jesus*

LEADING **YOUR KIDS** THE WAY CHRIST LED THE TWELVE

BARRETT JOHNSON

BETHANY HOUSE
a division of Baker Publishing Group
Minneapolis, Minnesota

© 2024 by Barrett Johnson

Published by Bethany House Publishers
Minneapolis, Minnesota
BethanyHouse.com

Bethany House Publishers is a division of
Baker Publishing Group, Grand Rapids, Michigan

Printed in the United States of America

Library of Congress Cataloging-in-Publication Data
Names: Johnson, Barrett, author.
Title: Disciple them like Jesus : leading your kids the way Christ led the twelve
    / Barrett Johnson.
Description: Minneapolis, Minnesota : Bethany House Publishers, a division of
    Baker Publishing Group, [2024] | Includes bibliographical references.
Identifiers: LCCN 2023058301 | ISBN 9780764243820 (paper) | ISBN
    9780764243943 (cloth) | ISBN 9781493448043 (ebook)
Subjects: LCSH: Child rearing—Religious aspects—Christianity. | Families—
    Religious aspects—Christianity. | Parenting—Religious aspects—Christianity.
Classification: LCC HQ768 .J54 2024 | DDC 248.8/45—dc23/eng/20240223
LC record available at https://lccn.loc.gov/2023058301

Cover design by Micah Kandros Design

Baker Publishing Group publications use paper produced from sustainable for-
estry practices and postconsumer waste whenever possible.

24   25   26   27   28   29   30   7   6   5   4   3   2   1

For Caleb, Carly, Katie Grace, Nalani, Olina, Rose, Lucy, and any other grandchildren God gives Jenifer and me in the future.

May your parents live out these truths
far better than we did.

Contents

Foreword

Do we really need another parenting book?

To be honest, I wasn't so sure when my husband, Barrett, set out to write this one. So many worthwhile resources are already out there offering direction to the Christian parent on a wide variety of issues and concerns. In fact, we own many of them, and we've even produced some ourselves. Yet we're all hard-pressed to find a resource that fundamentally, clearly, and simply defines the Christian parent's most foundational job.

For more than thirty years, I've been a mom in the trenches of raising our five kids and more recently providing some daily care for a few of our grandchildren. So I know how easy it is to become both distracted and exhausted by the mundane tasks of parenting. Sometimes I've just wanted to get through the day, far too easily losing sight of the big picture before me.

You're holding a big-picture book whose purpose is to clearly help you see what God calls you to prioritize as you parent your kids. It's a pretty short read that can be knocked out in a few hours, but for those of you who don't have even that much time to spare, let me give you the summary statement right up front:

Parenting is discipleship.

If you've been looking for meaning in the everyday monotony of parenting, assume that holding this book in your hands right now is a God-ordained moment. Assume that God wants you to wrap your mind around the fact that your primary role as a Christian parent is to join Him in developing your child into a fully devoted Christ-follower.

> *Your primary role as a Christian parent is to join God in developing your child into a fully devoted Christ-follower.*

This is the crux of disipleship. You have roughly twenty years to accomplish this goal with your kids, and the clock is ticking.

All that might sound a bit overwhelming. It does to me. But I encourage you to start taking baby steps, and this book will help you do exactly that. God just might use what's here to transform you into a more purposeful parent. If that happens, I'm confident that the children who come behind you will love Christ more deeply, obey Him more fully, and serve Him more effectively.

Still, the ultimate question remains, *How* do we become more purposeful parents? It certainly requires some measure of intentionality—and a ton of grace.

As a mom who stayed home with our children while Barrett worked as a youth and family minister in the local church, I feel like I did most of the heavy lifting of raising our kids.

And if I'm honest, I have to admit I tend to read parenting books written by men with a healthy dose of skepticism: *What does he know? He was peacefully writing in some quiet office while his wife was up to her neck in sweat, tears, and baby spit-up. What credibility does he have to tell me what I should be doing with my kids?*

Well, what you're about to read is credible because it's biblical. More than twenty years ago, while we were still struggling to make it through each day with our kids, Barrett came up with the basic structure of what he calls The Discipling Home. It was created as an hour-long presentation for the parents in our church, providing a clear picture of how Jesus discipled the twelve disciples and challenging parents to do likewise with their children. Essentially, this book is the lab result of two decades of our trying to put the priorities of Jesus into practice as we raised our own kids.

In the coming pages, you'll encounter a Christ-inspired paradigm that can help any parent stay focused on Jesus' command to make disciples, starting in their own homes. The Discipling Home model looks like this:

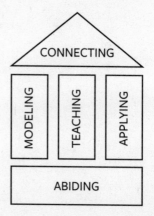

In the form of a house, these five words succinctly reflect the priorities and ways of Jesus, whom Scripture calls us to emulate. You'll hear Barrett say this a lot, but we truly believe discipling their children is a mom and dad's most important job.

At the end of each chapter, you'll have the opportunity to consider how you can best pursue this responsibility by answering questions and prompts in a section called "For Personal Reflection." You might want to pull out a journal or notebook to record your thoughts and personal prayers, which you can review later to see how far you've come—how God has answered your deepest desires as a parent.

Our hope for you, then, is that you'll ultimately stay focused on what Christ said is most important for everyone, including your children—discovering the joy found in an abundant life in Him. Jesus is rooting for you, and so am I. May God speak to you as you read!

—Jenifer Johnson,
Wife of the Author

one

PARENTING'S PRIMARY PURPOSE

Go and make disciples of all nations, baptizing them in the name of the Father and of the Son and of the Holy Spirit, and teaching them to obey everything I have commanded you. And surely I am with you always, to the very end of the age.

Jesus, Matthew 28:19–20

Let me first say this: I have no idea what I'm doing.

I've been a parent for thirty years, living three consecutive decades with children or teenagers in my home. And at this writing, I have four grown kids and a fifth moving through the challenges of adolescence. By and large, my children have turned out great. They're not perfect, but they love Jesus, love others, and are decent law-abiding citizens. People with kids younger than ours occasionally ask Jenifer and me, "How did you raise such great kids? What did you do? What's your secret?"

I don't know why our kids turned out the way they did. While I want to take some credit for who they are—as well as give props to their mother—I confess that for many years we were making it up as we went along. The reality is that the grace of God filled in a whole lot of gaps where we feel like we failed. We had some idea of what we were supposed to do, but that doesn't mean we always did it.

That may be suprising given that I'm a "professional Christian family man." That sounds strange, but I'm convinced that's how many people see me. After I served in the local church as a youth pastor and family minister for twenty-five years, Jenifer and I started a nonprofit family ministry. For the last decade, we've spoken to tens of thousands of people around the world about God's design for marriage, family, sexuality, and more. I'm supposedly an expert. In the words of one arrogant (and fictional) anchorman, "I'm kind of a big deal. . . . People know me. . . . I'm very important."[1]

But just because I'm an "expert" doesn't mean I always know what I'm doing. I've done my best to raise my five kids with God-given purpose, but many days I'm not so sure how well I did. Like every other parent, even "professionals" like me, I question if I have what it takes. Then life throws a curveball, and that question grows even louder.

As I write these words, I'm in the early days of fighting a rare and aggressive cancer. As you can imagine, this diagnosis has caused me to reflect on a whole litany of regrets. I find myself thinking of all the things I should've, could've, and would've done and would change if I had the chance to live those decades over again. And you can be sure I've questioned how I've fulfilled my role as a parent.

But if I could start all over as a dad, what would I do differently? Without a doubt I'd be more intentional in leading and guiding my kids to fall in love with Jesus and follow Him wherever He leads them. Everything else in their lives—character, relationships, education, career—is dependent on their personal relationships with God. So I will argue that our most important job as parents is helping our children follow Jesus. If they get that right, we can be confident that their lives will be blessed.

While that sounds like an ideal target for a Christian parent to aim for, I realize there's both bad news and good news. The bad news is that the path our children ultimately choose to take is completely up to them; we can't make their choices for them. The good news is that we have a couple of decades to present the options to them more clearly than anyone else in their lives can.

At its core, then, this book is about a parent's—or even a grandparent's—power to help make a child's choice to follow Jesus a no-brainer. But taking responsibility to use that power can feel overwhelming given the burden we already feel: believing we must somehow be perfect parents.

Can we all agree that parenting in today's world is incredibly hard? When we talk to parents around the country, a common theme emerges: the pressure to raise kids who turn out right feels heavier than ever. I don't think our parents' generation was nearly as stressed-out about this as we are, and a post on Facebook a few years ago perfectly and humorously captured that idea:

How To Be A Mom in 2017: Make sure your children's academic, emotional, psychological, mental, spiritual, physical, nutritional, and social needs are met while being careful not to overstimulate, understimulate, improperly medicate, helicopter, or neglect them in a screen-free, processed foods-free, GMO-free, negative energy-free, plastic-free, body positive, socially conscious, egalitarian but also authoritative, nurturing but fostering of independence, gentle but not overly permissive, pesticide-free two-story, multilingual home preferably in a cul-de-sac with a backyard and 1.5 siblings spaced at least two year[s] apart for proper development also don't forget the coconut oil.

How To Be A Mom In Literally Every Generation Before Ours: Feed them sometimes.[2]

Perhaps you can relate. With all this pressure on us, pulling us in each and every direction, it's easy to lose sight of what we're supposed to be doing as parents. Everyone seems to have a different opinion about what our priorities should be, and listening to all those messages can be exhausting, causing us to question whether we're doing anything right. On top of that, add the guilt that comes from comparing our home lives to the perfectly curated families we see on our social media streams. Ultimately, all this can leave us feeling like failures as parents.

> *This book is about a parent's—or even a grandparent's—power to make a child's choice to follow Jesus a no-brainer.*

Does God intend for us to feel confusion and even paralysis from such a lack of focus? No. I'm confident that He wants us to parent with purpose, that He desires us to live each day knowing He has an agenda for our homes. The key is for us to keep sight of what that agenda is.

A Parable on the Importance of Knowing Your Purpose

A parable might help us all understand how easy it is to lose sight of what really matters. This one—which Louie Giglio once told and is paraphrased here with his permission—is a bit long, but it drives home a valuable reality. I encourage you to stick with it.

There once was a young entrepreneur who inherited a significant amount of money. Looking for a business in which to invest, he came across a company that manufactured rubber tubing. Though it had been in operation for more than forty years, production was down, employee morale was low, and the company was in serious trouble. Due to the mundane nature of the work, the people just could not get excited about making rubber tubing! Confident he could turn the company around, he bought it and quickly put together a plan to re-vitalize production.

On the first Monday after purchasing the business, the seventy-five employees arrived at work to discover the factory closed and their new boss standing in front of two buses in the parking lot. Once everyone was present, he instructed them to climb aboard the buses for a required field trip. Confused but curious, the men and women piled onto the buses and settled into their seats.

After a thirty-minute drive, they found themselves at the city's international airport, bypassing the terminals and heading to a large maintenance hangar at the edge of a runway. The buses stopped in front of a 727 parked on the tarmac. Once they all piled out of the buses and gathered around the plane, the new owner climbed to the top of the access stairs and asked them all to come aboard.

Confused even more, the employees obeyed. Once they all found seats, the owner said over the loudspeaker, "A flight attendant will now share some of the safety features of this airplane."

The flight attendant immediately began the typical pre-flight safety lecture, explaining how to buckle the seat belts, the location of all the exits, and how oxygen masks would drop from the ceiling in an emergency. Many of the employees buckled their seat belts, thinking perhaps their new boss was taking them on an unexpected trip.

Once the familiar presentation was over, the flight attendant took her seat, and the plane grew quiet. The next few minutes passed slowly as the employees sat in a state of bewilderment. Some fidgeted in their seats or whispered quietly to those beside them, "What in the world are we doing here?"

Then on a discreet cue given by the new owner, a technician pulled the lever that releases the oxygen masks from the ceiling. The masks immediately dropped, just as they're designed to do. After the initial surprise (and a few jittery people actually fitting the masks to their faces), the employees again sat in confusion, staring at the oxygen units hanging just in front of their noses.

Another few minutes slowly ticked by until, without warning, a twenty-five-year veteran of the company yelled from the back of the plane, "Hey! I know this stuff!" He was joyously holding the oxygen unit in his hand. "This is our six millimeter clear silicone tubing!"

The other employees grabbed their oxygen masks and examined them. As they looked closely, they noticed their company name and logo were lightly marked along the length of tube. Congratulatory cheers went up, and high fives were exchanged among many in the cabin.

Once the group settled down, the owner's voice once again came over the loudspeaker. "Our company has been the world's leading supplier of silicone tubing to the airline industry for the past twenty years. More than 3,500 commercial planes in the air today utilize our tubing in their emergency oxygen systems. In the past two decades, these have been used more than fifteen hundred times during flight, saving the lives of more than one hundred thousand people."

Then after a dramatic pause, he said, "Please get back on the buses."

The buses then transported the group to a well-known university hospital. Inside, they were escorted into the large balcony of a surgical theater, where an open-heart operation was about to begin. Once the patient was anesthetized and hooked up to the heart-lung machine, the procedure began. Understandably, some of the employees were uncomfortable. Still, the company's new owner encouraged them to carefully watch what was happening.

After a few minutes, a buzz began to pass through the men and women of the company. The owner smiled when he saw that they recognized the ten millimeter surgical tube circulating the patient's blood through the heart-lung machine as their own. Their smiles of pride were exactly what he'd been hoping for.

Loud enough for the somber group to hear, he whispered, "At present, 35 percent of the world's twenty thousand heart-lung machines are equipped with our tubing. We've built a significant market share because our product is the best. It's helped sustain the lives of some six million heart patients over the past twenty-five years. Six million."

He paused to let the significance of that number sink in, then said, "I would love to see us do more of the same in the future."

Then he asked them to quietly leave the hospital and take their seats on the buses.

Before finally returning to their factory that evening, the little convoy of buses made brief stops at the research and development lab of a cutting-edge pharmaceutical company and at an automotive assembly plant. The employees saw more examples of how their tubing was effectively utilized in valuable ways.

Each location they visited filled them with a greater and greater understanding of the importance of their work. They weren't just manufacturing rubber tubing; they were creating a product essential to sustaining life and adding significant value to their world. Knowing the result of their labor restored in them a renewed commitment to excellence, even in the often-mundane work at their factory.

In the days and months that followed, company morale skyrocketed, production increased dramatically, and sales went through the roof all because the employees envisioned the results of their labor. Each spool of tubing they shipped was created with a renewed enthusiasm and immense satisfaction in their work. And it all happened by keeping their ultimate objective in the center of their focus.

The Moral of the Story

Along most of the twenty-year process of raising even one child, average parents find themselves taking on the same mundane and occasionally mind-numbing responsibilities over and over again:

- Changing many thousands of stinky, dirty diapers
- Dealing with innumerable interrupted or entirely sleepless nights
- Brushing baby teeth, clipping little nails, bathing squirmy bodies, and reading favorite bedtime stories for the umpteenth time
- Mastering the art of making peanut butter and jelly sandwiches (and cutting it crosswise or diagonal or whatever way your child wants it that day)
- Playing beginner kids' games like Candy Land and Chutes and Ladders or whatever game a preschooler makes up and thinks is the best game ever
- Buying jeans and shoes more than once a year (because just how fast can one kid grow?)
- Driving to playdates, school, practices, doctor and dentist appointments, and dozens of other places you never even thought about before you had kids
- Enduring homework battles and helping with last-minute school projects (what store with poster board and fresh markers is closest?)

The list goes on and on. If we're not careful, parenthood can be just an extremely long series of exhausting tasks, repeated over and over, ad nauseam. It can feel as boring and monotonous as working on an assembly line that makes rubber tubing.

Without focus and a clear awareness of our basic goal, the tendency is to get stuck in the rituals of daily life and forget that God has placed us in a totally unique situation with an essential mandate. Specifically, we're called to disciple our children. And again, without a doubt, this is a parent's most important job.

We're tasked with preparing our kids to know Jesus and walk intimately with Him. Over the course of a couple of decades, we're to help them join God in His mission of bringing redemption and salvation to a world separated from their creator. We're charged with helping the little people in our homes get caught up in God's amazing plan for their lives. This is the fundamental and only nonnegotiable spiritual purpose of parenting in the Christian home.

Yet the pressures of our busy schedules and the routine cycles of life can easily distract us, resulting in this critical task getting lost in the mayhem. Without a clear sense of purpose, it's easy to lose sight of the objective. Just as workers on a rubber tubing assembly line can forget their work has meaning, so, too, can we forget that the daily work of parenting a child has the potential to create a committed follower of Jesus Christ.

One who just might change the world.

Perhaps it's easy to lose sight of this calling because the process takes so long and we see so few significant milestones along the journey. With most any other endeavor, we have the satisfaction of receiving regular feedback on our progress in the form of small successes and victories. In school we get periodic report cards. At work we might finish projects or close deals. Even in our church activities, we can conclude and then evaluate events or programs.

Parenting is a different animal altogether. You get very little feedback. When was the last time your children let you know your contribution to their lives is invaluable? Or your peers or your own parents commented on your success as a parent? It rarely happens. Likewise, with the exception of events like a profession of faith or baptism, it's hard to know day by day or even year by year just how your kids are growing spiritually. Like their physical growth, your kids' spiritual growth is likely to be so gradual that you might barely notice it except when God opens your eyes to some dramatic step they've taken.

It's possible that you won't be able to truly evaluate your success as a parent until, after eighteen years or so, you launch your child into independence and young adulthood. At that point, it can seem too late to have any meaningful impact on their spiritual trajectory. (But that's not necessarily the case, and we'll talk about that later.)

Making Disciples Is the Main Reason We're Here

Jesus made it clear that this world is not our home. From the time we're adopted into His family, we live the rest of our lives aware that we don't quite fit in on planet Earth. We were made to worship and honor God with everything we have and are, and every day we live here is full of reminders that we truly don't belong.

In my way of thinking, it would make complete sense for every new convert to Christ to be immediately transported to heaven—just like they used to beam people up to the USS *Enterprise* on *Star Trek*. After all, heaven is our home! We were made to worship and adore God for eternity, so why delay the very thing we were designed to do?

Still, God chooses not to "beam us up" when we become His followers. This, then, begs the question, Why does He leave us here when it's obvious that we were made for something so much better? The answer is that He leaves us here with an assignment. He's commanded us to share what we know of Jesus with a lost and dying world in hopes of drawing others to Him.

And that's why He charged His disciples with what we now know as the Great Commission:

> Go and make disciples of all nations, baptizing them in the name of the Father and of the Son and of the Holy Spirit, and teaching them to obey everything I have commanded you. And surely I am with you always, to the very end of the age.
>
> Matthew 28:19–20

Immediately before returning to heaven, Christ gave a clear directive telling His followers what they were to do: make disciples. He was essentially telling them, "Just as I've taught you to follow Me and align your lives completely with My agenda, I want you to now go and do likewise. Tell people about Me and My gospel. Integrate them into fellowship through baptism. Teach them to obey all the things I've taught you."

Fundamentally, discipleship is helping people know, love, and follow Jesus.

Fundamentally, discipleship is helping people know, love, and follow Jesus.

Nothing has changed in two thousand years. Our primary objective remains the same. Discipleship is still the reason we're here. But tragically, many believers are far more committed to building their own kingdoms than to building the kingdom of God. Furthermore, too many who recognize God's command to make disciples have failed to give attention to the most obvious target for their efforts: their own children.

Parents Are the Most Strategically Placed Disciple-Makers in God's Creation

Many churches take the "baptizing them" part of the Great Commission very seriously but fail miserably with the "teaching them to obey" part. This is because conversion usually happens quickly, but discipleship is a slow, challenging process taking place throughout a believer's entire lifetime. Investing in another person for a few years or even a few months can be hard work, and too few of the busy people in our churches are truly committed to helping new believers grow in the faith.

As parents, we have an incredible opportunity to disciple the children God has placed in our homes. And He's made it simple. On the one hand is a child who needs to be introduced to Christ and then grown up in the faith. On the other hand is a committed adult believer who's been given the command to make disciples. God creates something of a captive audience by, in His sovereign will, placing one in the home of the other for twenty years or so. He makes the child dependent on the parent, giving the adult many opportunities to teach, shape, and mold the child. What a perfectly simple plan for growing new believers!

Yet, again, too many parents miss this opportunity. The most common mindset I've observed is their leaving the spiritual development of their children to the church. We've somehow come to believe that if we take our children to Sunday school or get our teenagers involved in a youth program, we've made the greatest possible contribution to their spiritual growth and development.

How tragic! Not to mention unbiblical. While the church should certainly be a resource for Christian parents, it should never be the primary means by which their children are discipled. In fact, it can't be. And yet many of us still count on the church to help our kids encounter Christ and learn to walk with Him. While the church should reinforce what we're doing at home, God has given the primary responsibility for the spiritual development of children to parents. Again, taking ownership of this role may feel overwhelming; it's a heavy burden. But it's an essential one for every mom and dad.

I realize how scary this might sound—even worse than overwhelming. It may seem like this is just one more dimension of parenting where you could potentially end up feeling like a failure. Take heart! The goal of this book is to make meeting this central responsibility of parenting as clear and easy as possible. The model you'll find in the next chapter will hopefully inform, challenge, and resource you to move forward with peace of mind, knowing you're joining God in His big agenda for your kids. You'll feel encouraged, not overwhelmed or scared.

One thing is certain: if you want to make a difference in the world, the best place to start is with your children. The legacy of faith you'll pass down from one generation to the next has a multiplication power with the potential to literally change the world. Don't believe me? Consider my family as an example:

Phase 1

Jenifer and I have five children, and we've done our best to teach them the ways of Jesus. Hopefully, they'll stay committed to Him and look for opportunities to be used by Him throughout their lives.

Phase 2

No guarantees, but let's assume that every one of our five children marries. Including their spouses, then, Jenifer and I would have ten young adults to pour our lives into.

Phase 3

This is a stretch, but what if each of our kids and their spouses have five kids like we did? They probably won't, but just for fun, let's imagine they do. How many grandchildren would Jenifer and I have? Twenty-five. If each of those kids went on to marry, we would have fifty young adults to pour Jesus into. Hopefully, their parents (our kids) would encourage them to be used by God as well.

Phase 4 and Beyond

Now let's say all that happened for another generation. Using those same admittedly crazy numbers in this day and age, Jenifer and I could potentially have 125 great-grandchildren. If we continue to include their spouses, that's 250 people our lives would have directly impacted. The numbers keep growing, and the impact of each generation taught and discipled to follow Jesus would have a greater and greater impact.

Two Hundred Years after Phase 1

If you play out that same pattern for eight generations (and include our descendants' spouses), then in about two hundred years (at twenty-five years per generation), do you know how many descendants Jenifer and I could have? Nearly one million. *One. Million.* That's a *one* followed by *six zeros*.

Can you even begin to quantify the potential kingdom impact of a million committed Christ-followers? How might God use them to affect their communities and the churches where they serve? How might God use the vast money and resources they'd have and share to be a blessing to the world? How might God use even a small percentage of them (which might be tens of thousands) as missionaries or to do humanitarian work in the name of Christ?

My short life might be meaningful, but the potentially vast impact of the generations that come behind me is absolutely immeasurable. Granted, my everybody-have-five-kids dream isn't reasonable, but this truth remains: God can greatly multiply the fruit of any spiritual investment I make into my children and grandchildren. This is because who I lead them to become will be passed on to future generations.

As the late Christian communicator Steve Farrar once said, "I may not know my great-great-grandchildren, but my great-great-grandchildren will know me."[3] They will know each of us through what we pass on to our children.

Consider this question: what legacy will you leave on this earth? Could the greatest impact you make in the kingdom be to multiply yourself in your children, launching them into the great adventure of knowing and serving God? That's exactly what Jesus did with His disciples. And it will do us well to consider exactly how He did it and what we can learn from His example.

As you read on, ask God to show you what you can learn not just from the teachings of Christ but also from the example of disciple-making He gave us to follow.

FOR PERSONAL *Reflection*

- "Parenting is discipleship." Is this a new concept for you? If not, where have you heard it before? How did it impact you then? How does it impact you now?

- Have you seen the spiritual development of your kids as one of your many parenting objectives? Or as the main job God has given you as a parent? Which do you think it is? Why? And if you could ask God how He would answer that question, what do you think He would say?

- Does the responsibility of discipling your kids bring out any emotions in you? Do you feel overwhelmed? Scared? Challenged? Empowered? In each case, why or why not?
- Have you observed any parents you know being intentional in the spiritual growth of their kids? What do you think you could emulate in them? What do they do right?
- Ask God to begin stirring in you a clear picture of the ultimate goals and objectives He has for the children He's entrusted to you. Ask Him to show you where your goals and His goals don't align and how to best address that gap.

two

DISCIPLE LIKE JESUS

If you can't see where you are going, ask someone who has been there before.

J. Loren Norris[1]

Though it's a hobby far too expensive in both money and time for me to pursue on a regular basis, I like to play golf. That's why I jump at the few opportunities I get to spend four or five hours hitting and then chasing a little white ball. And I really do enjoy it. If I have an early morning tee time, I toss and turn all night, unable to sleep because of the anticipation I have for the coming day.

As much as I love to play the game, though, let me make one thing clear: I'm a horrible golfer. I know few people as consistently inconsistent in the game as I am. Oh, I've tried to improve. Unlike most golfers I know, I actually welcome the tips my well-meaning friends give me in the middle of one of my typical one-hundred-stroke rounds. Tips like:

"Keep your head down."
"Don't chicken-wing your arms."
"Slow down your backswing."

I've even taken a few lessons, though I'm not sure they'll ever make a difference unless I get out and practice more. But again, due to the expense of time and money, that's just not going to happen.

Yet I've come up with the ultimate solution for transforming me into an incredible golfer. It's not a very realistic plan, but here it is:

I'd study the golf swing and technique of a skilled golfer in perfect detail and then teach my body to exactly copy what I observed. For example, I'd study Tiger Woods, one of the greatest golfers of all time.

I know this is a mythical stretch of my imagination, but stick with me. Obviously, in my pursuit of Tiger-esque golf, I would need to commit to getting in top physical shape (as he likely was at the peak of his game) so I could have a similar body strength to draw from. Tiger and I are about the same height, so perhaps that's possible.

Then at the most detailed level, I'd observe the elements of how he does what he does to hit a golf ball. I would examine every dimension of his swing in every conceivable situation. I'd become the absolute expert on his game, committing every part of it to memory. Then I would copy him exactly. All this might take a lifetime of coaching and practice, but it's theoretically possible that I could become as technically excellent as Tiger.

Then I would just need to acquire his judgment, develop his competitive spirit, and gain his experience. I'm confident that if I could consistently and accurately imitate Tiger Woods—at least on the golf course—I'd become a pretty successful golfer.

There's a broader truth hidden in my golf-improvement fantasy. The greatest key to learning something new or developing something in yourself is to find someone to emulate. Once you identify a person who already does it well, you have a target at which to aim.

> *The greatest key to learning something new or developing something in yourself is to find someone to emulate.*

If we want to know how to make disciples—particularly those in our own homes—then the best place to start is by carefully examining the greatest disciple-maker of all time: Jesus Christ. Then we have the opportunity to disciple like He did.

What Did Jesus Do?

At some point in our lives, we've all considered the question *What would Jesus do?* It's a good question to pose. (And an easily marketable one! How many WWJD bracelets did you own back in the nineties?) Asking this question does have inherent risks, though, because anybody can infer or imagine what Jesus would do in any given situation based on their own beliefs about Him. But those beliefs may or may not be grounded in Scripture. So for our purposes here, let's consider not what Jesus *would* do but what He *did* do, particularly as it pertains to discipleship.

Jesus spent three years investing Himself in twelve ordinary guys: a handful of fishermen, some blue-collar workers, a few faithful yet fickle men from John the Baptist's entourage. They were certainly nothing special. But Jesus was. And who He was made an impact on them in a powerful way. After He returned to the Father, these men were able to carry on His ministry, establish the church, and change the course of history. Based on the results alone, we know they were well equipped for the task.

So how did Jesus do it? How did He prepare them for the life to which He was calling them?

The answer is found by carefully considering Jesus and the disciples' priorities and activities in Scripture's four Gospels—Matthew, Mark, Luke, and John. And while Christ certainly didn't adhere to any specific discipleship program you might find in your local church, we can identify five key components of His discipleship strategy. These components are the basis for The Discipling Home model we'll examine more deeply in the coming chapters.

1. Jesus Stayed Close to His Heavenly Father

Jesus knew He could do nothing without the Father's presence, power, and blessing, so He placed the greatest of priorities upon maintaining intimacy with Him. Jesus made that clear with these words: "I and the Father are one" (John 10:30).

We could take off on an enormous tangent here by discussing the full meaning of Jesus' words, the nature of the Trinity, and the theological implications of the triune Godhead. But I'll leave that important issue to another book and those more qualified than me. For our purposes here it's only important to recognize that throughout His ministry Jesus remained close to God. So close, in fact, that He didn't distinguish between His actions and God's actions, between His thoughts and God's thoughts. He truly was in perfect unity with His Father. And this was the foundational element of all He said and did.

2. Jesus Modeled the Life He Desired His Disciples to Lead

The first tangible result of Jesus' intimacy with the Father was that He served as a crystal-clear example of a life that's pleasing to God. The disciples had to look no further than Jesus Himself to see what obedience, faith, joy, and love in action look like. That's what made Him so magnetic to His followers (and even to many of those who didn't follow Him). In John 13:34 we read that Jesus said, "A new command I give you: Love one another. As I have loved you, so you must love one another."

Jesus built His ministry and His disciples' training around this premise: *Do what I do*. In an era dominated by the Pharisees and their double-talk, contradiction, and dead religion, Jesus arrived on the scene as someone entirely credible, someone who perfectly walked His talk. This was an essential component of His process of leading the disciples.

3. Jesus Taught His Disciples the Ways of God

Perhaps above all else, throughout His ministry Jesus was known as a great teacher. Even outside the church, our world has a reverent respect for what Jesus had to say. That people can deny His deity yet recognize great truth in His words speaks volumes. And while we can read some recorded teachings of Christ in the four Gospels, those in Jesus' inner circle likely had the privilege of an intensive three-year kingdom education.

Today, someone could sit and read all four Gospels cover to cover, taking in all of Jesus' recorded teachings in a single afternoon. That might be the equivalent of one intense day of teaching, giving that person a tremendous amount of food for thought. But can you imagine all the disciples heard in three years of life spent with Christ? The apostle John wrote,

"If every one of [the things Jesus did] were written down, I suppose that even the whole world would not have room for the books that would be written" (John 21:25).

From the moment Jesus began His Sermon on the Mount with the words *Blessed are the*, His followers discovered that this new life in Him would be different. While in Christ's life they could see what kingdom living was to look like, they were also taught the nuts and bolts of finding their own place in God's activity on earth. He taught them how to love, follow, and obey their heavenly Father. And He taught them much about how to love the people with whom they interacted every day.

4. Jesus Gave His Disciples Opportunities to Apply What He Taught Them

Perhaps the most important component in Jesus' plan to prepare the disciples for life without His physical presence was their on-the-job training. Unlike too many teachers, Jesus gave His disciples the chance to put into practice what He was modeling and teaching:

These twelve Jesus sent out with the following instructions: "Do not go among the Gentiles or enter any town of the Samaritans. Go rather to the lost sheep of Israel. As you go, proclaim this message: 'The kingdom of heaven has come near.' Heal the sick, raise the dead, cleanse those who have leprosy, drive out demons. Freely you have received; freely give."

Matthew 10:5–8

The disciples were sent out to do ministry without Him but always with the knowledge that He was close by to coach them along. As they encountered the difficulties and tasted the victories of kingdom work, Jesus was there to ensure the right lessons were learned. No doubt, the more they did with Him, the more comfortable they became with the prospect of doing it all without Him. In other words, they learned to stand on their own. (And after the Holy Spirit showed up in Acts 2, there was no stopping them.)

5. Jesus Did Everything with His Disciples in the Context of a Relationship

I don't get the impression that Jesus devoted Himself to leading His disciples during a set time each week. In fact, Scripture gives us the impression that He and the Twelve spent every day together for three intense *years*.

In everyday moments of eating, playing, talking, laughing, and working together, they were able to develop the intimate relationship that made powerful discipleship possible. It transcended the typical teacher-student relationship we're used to. Jesus said to them, "I no longer call you servants, because a servant does not know his master's business. Instead, I have called you friends, for everything that I learned from my Father I have made known to you" (John 15:15).

Jesus called His disciples His friends, and we can assume that's exactly what they were. Their hearts were knit closely together, creating the ideal environment for Jesus to do in them exactly what His heavenly Father desired. Without this love relationship, true and lasting life change in the twelve disciples would have been impossible.

These five elements are the five main priorities Jesus established in His role as disciple-maker to the twelve men in His inner circle. Though it's certainly not an exhaustive list, I believe we can place any of His priorities into one of these five categories. They were all critical, even essential. And the results speak for themselves.

These five elements can and should serve as a pattern to follow as we disciple our children. Following Jesus' example, they can help us grasp and maintain the big picture of our responsibility as Christian parents.

We All Need Direction

God's call to disciple our kids is more important and more critical than anything else we'll do as parents, yet as we've already noted, it's easy to lose sight of this priority. With all the cultural pressures and worldly values coming to bear on our lives, we need direction. We can't minimize the power and significance of a clearly defined model to provide guidance in the midst of all the potential distractions.

It's sort of like the build-it-yourself furniture I furnished my house with in the early days of marriage. You know, those miscellaneous bookshelves, TV stands, end tables, and so on made of particle board material far heavier than lead and guaranteed to hold its genuine imitation wood grain appearance for at least six months.

The instruction booklet that came with the furniture was invaluable to the assembly process—even if it didn't have any words. The small step-by-step diagrams helped me build the furniture as designed. On the other hand, if I ignored the diagrams, the result was frustration and confusion. While any detailed instructions like that are certainly welcome, the greatest value was in the simple pictures that modeled what I was building.

When it comes to raising children, there's no clear-cut manual, no step-by-step instructions on how to properly prepare our kids for God's best for their lives. Jenifer used to reflect on how God answered our prayer for children by giving us our first three kids in four years. Then she found herself sitting on the floor surrounded by our precious gifts from God without a clue as to what to do with them.

I'm sure most parents have moments like this—feeling overwhelmed by the responsibility of raising a child. It often happens during those first few days after bringing a baby home from the hospital, but it can hit us at many of the stages along the parent-child relationship journey. While at times we can feel ill-equipped for the task, other times we can feel overwhelmed with the number of possible instructions available to us.

For example, we start with all the lessons—good and bad—we learned from our parents and our own value systems of right and wrong. We load ourselves up with helpful books and resources. We might also seek direction for how to raise our kids from well-meaning friends. Add to that the brief bursts of information we get from social media, and we can be absolutely overwhelmed with options.

What we really need is direction from the God who loves us and has amazing plans for our kids. We need a simple model to help us sort out all the mind-numbing noise and keep us focused on God's call to discipleship as we raise our children.

That's what we're introducing here: a simple Christ-centered model that serves as the outline for the rest of what you'll read in this book. And like the diagram that helps me assemble a piece of furniture, this model will hopefully keep your parenting objectives clear.

> *We need a simple model to help us sort out all the mind-numbing noise and keep us focused on God's call to discipleship as we raise our children.*

No model is perfect, and this one certainly is not. Still, I sincerely hope it enables you to clearly see a process for discipling your children. As with the rubber tubing employees in our first chapter parable, if you're not clearly focused on the outcome, an effective process will never develop.

My prayer is that this model will help you conceptualize both the ways of Jesus and a tangible means by which you can grow your children in the faith.

The Discipling Home

The five components of our discipleship paradigm are each based on one of the five values demonstrated in the life of Jesus as He equipped His disciples (see pages 39–43). Their essence can be captured by the following five words:

Abiding
Modeling
Teaching
Applying
Connecting

These five components will be examined more deeply in the coming five chapters. But for our purposes here, the model is most clearly expressed in the form of a house. The house diagram works at both a functional level and at a symbolic level. Functionally, it works because the model has a foundation, three key pillars, and a roof. Each of the five elements is necessary to create a complete, stable structure. Symbolically, it serves as a reminder that discipleship begins at home.

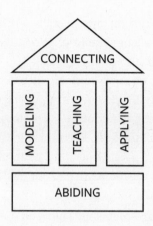

The Foundation—Abiding: Walking with God

If Jesus stayed connected to His heavenly Father, then any parent who desires to disciple their kids will want to start there too. This foundation established first in our lives enables us to accomplish everything else that matters.

Jesus drove home the importance of this foundation when He said to all of us, "I am the vine, you are the branches; the one who remains in Me, and I in him bears much fruit, for apart from Me you can do nothing" (John 15:5 NASB).

This world has many well-read, well-meaning parents who trust in their experience and know-how to guide them as they raise their children. But in no uncertain terms Jesus let us know our skill and commitment to parenting are irrelevant if we're not closely connected to Him. He doesn't see abiding in

Him as a necessary component to move you from pretty good parenting to excellent parenting. He sees it as foundational to your accomplishing anything at all.

Without Him, we can do nothing. Zilch. Zero. Nada. If we're not walking with Christ, then we're trusting in our flesh, and my understanding of Scripture is that nothing of eternal value comes from the flesh. Everything in Christian parenting hinges on the parent's personal relationship with God. That's why it's at the foundation of our model.

The First Pillar—Modeling: Living an Authentic Christian Life

If Jesus clearly modeled the life He desired His disciples to lead, then leading by example will be a nonnegotiable in our lives as well. It takes its place as the first of three essential pillars in our model. In the same way Jesus did, modeling an authentic Christian faith and lifestyle is the first value we must choose to commit ourselves to as parents.

The apostle Paul showed the value of modeling as he developed disciples in the churches he helped build. In his letter to the church at Philippi, he offers himself as an example of how to live and be: "Whatever you have learned or received or heard from me, or seen in me—put it into practice. And the God of peace will be with you" (Philippians 4:9).

His point was this: "If you're unsure about what to do, how to act, how to think, and so on, then look no further than my example. Sure, do the things I've taught you. But more importantly, do the things you've seen in me." Because your children know you better than anyone, leading by example is essential to discipling them. You can fool just about everyone else in your life, but you can't fool your kids. They know you too well.

The Second Pillar—Teaching: Pointing Your Children to the Truth

We know Jesus taught His disciples how to know, love, and follow God. And if we're to follow His example, then teaching our children the nuts and bolts of Christian living and biblical thinking is our second essential component.

The children of Israel were given the following command as an essential step in growing their children in the faith:

> These commandments that I give you today are to be upon your hearts. Impress them on your children. Talk about them when you sit at home and when you walk along the road, when you lie down and when you get up. Tie them as symbols on your hands and bind them on your foreheads. Write them on the doorframes of your houses and on your gates.
>
> Deuteronomy 6:6–9

In our digital media culture, our kids are constantly bombarded with the world's lies. They're being indoctrinated without even knowing it. If the eternal truths of God have any hope of infiltrating and impacting our world, then they must pass from one generation to the next. And God gives this essential responsibility to parents. We have the opportunity to take a proactive role in this teaching process, just as Jesus did with His disciples.

The Third Pillar—Applying: Giving Your Children Opportunities to Live Out Their Faith

Jesus gave His disciples opportunities to put what they learned into practice. Likewise, if we teach our children to know the truth but don't give them chances to apply it, then we've neglected this third essential component. We deny them the privilege of experiencing God for themselves.

Many well-meaning parents do a great job of modeling the life of a Christian and teaching the truth yet fail to pass on a lasting faith to their children. That's because the kids never have a chance to actually put what they've learned into practice for themselves. James warned us against the pitfalls of knowledge without action: "Do not merely listen to the word, and so deceive yourselves. Do what it says" (James 1:22).

If we learn the ways of the Lord but it doesn't result in a changed life, we're fooling ourselves. We've missed the point altogether. In the process of discipling our children, we get to give them greater and greater opportunities to live out their faith as they grow and mature in their understanding of the

Christian life. If all they have is head knowledge and never actually experience God at work in their lives, they'll never "taste and see that the LORD is good" (Psalm 34:8).

The Roof—Connecting: Developing and Maintaining a Love Relationship with Your Children

Finally, Jesus did all He did in the context of relationship with His disciples. We can do likewise. Just as a house with no roof makes for an incomplete dwelling, our discipleship model isn't complete without a growing, vibrant love relationship with our children.

The apostle Paul captured this sentiment perfectly in his letter to the church at Thessalonica: "Because we loved you so much, we were delighted to share with you not only the gospel of God but our lives as well" (1 Thessalonians 2:8).

The great motivator for Paul, and certainly for those he taught and led, was the intense love between them. It's so easy for parents to slip into an attitude that says *My children should do what I say simply because I say so.* While God has placed children in a role submissive to their parents, the main propellant for growth and maturity should be love, not simply obedience. We only have to look to Jesus' example to see that truth lived out. If anyone merited obedience, it was Christ. Yet He dealt with His disciples not as His servants but as His friends. If we're to follow His example in discipleship, we'll do the same with our children.

Consider Jesus' Discipleship Model

Take time to consider Jesus' discipleship model. Prayerfully meditate on how and why He did what He did with those twelve men who were closest to Him. Consider making a new commitment to both follow Christ more closely and to transfer what He did with His followers to what you will do with those who are following after you.

As you work through the next five chapters, you'll have the chance to consider more carefully each of the five components of Jesus' model. Ideally, you'll see how each one plays a crucial role—not one of them is optional or expendable. The model will collapse and the spiritual development of our children will suffer if all five components are not in place.

These five priorities will be developed in order from bottom to top, just as one might build a house. But they're not meant to be introduced in your family in sequential order. It's not like you master one before moving on to another. Instead, just as Jesus consistently personified each of these five components simultaneously, that should be your goal as well.

Sure, God may convict you of certain things to address or focus on in any given season of your family life. But overall, this process will require some measure of multitasking. Don't worry. God is with you and promises to help you. Since the beginning of time, His agenda has been for your kids to follow Him. He will never leave you to figure this out on your own. He is near, so you have what it takes!

My hope and prayer is that you realize that while the task of discipling your kids might feel overwhelming, it *is* possible. Keeping this clear model of Christ's example in your heart and mind can give eternal purpose to your everyday family life. With all the pressure we're under with our modern-day busyness, we parents desperately need this help and direction.

FOR PERSONAL
Reflection

- What does being a disciple of Jesus mean to you? What did it mean to the disciples Jesus called? Is there a difference?
- Have you ever considered Jesus as an example of how you can parent with purpose? What might it mean to parent like Jesus in your family?
- How are you doing with each of these five components of discipleship with your kids? Give yourself a quick letter grade here or in a notebook or journal:

  Abiding: Walking with God
  Modeling: Living an Authentic Christian Life
  Teaching: Pointing Your Children to the Truth

Applying: Giving Your Children Opportunities to Live Out Their Faith

Connecting: Developing and Maintaining a Love Relationship with Your Children

- Ask God to begin filling in the gaps where you believe you're currently weak. He promises to help you create an environment in your home where each family member can become more and more like Jesus.

three

ABIDING

Walking with God

Jesus taught that your highest priority must be your relationship with Him. If anything detracts you from that relationship, that activity is not from God. God will not ask you to do something that hinders your relationship with Christ.

Henry Blackaby[1]

When our kids were young, we moved from Houston to Fort Worth. In our desperate search for a home, we found a great deal on a huge house that had been in foreclosure proceedings for more than a year. The house was in terrible shape, but we knew we could fix it up and make it uniquely ours. So we offered $15,000 less than the already low price the bank was asking, and they jumped on it. We were ecstatic!

As young homebuyers, though, we didn't think through one thing: we hadn't yet sold our home in Houston, and we couldn't secure a mortgage until we did. Not wanting to see this great deal get away from us, our new church secured a temporary loan for us through a few kind and generous members.

We made a quick deal with the bank, and after closing we speedily replaced every floor, countertop, and light and plumbing fixture. We also painted every surface in the entire interior and exterior of the house. Finally, after about six frantic weeks of cosmetic renovations, we moved into what felt like a brand-new place.

When we finally sold our house in Houston and were able to apply for a mortgage, a full home inspection revealed that the Fort Worth house's foundation was sloping rather significantly in the twenty feet from the kitchen to the garage. No wonder the bank wanted to sell it so fast and cheap!

In nearly a decade of living there, we never spent the big bucks to rep
air the foundation like we probably should have. Instead, we dealt with cracked kitchen tiles, splits in the Sheetrock, and small gaps in the exterior brick. (Our young kids also got the thrill of watching marbles roll independently down the hall near our kitchen. Bonus!)

We sold the house when we moved to Atlanta, giving full disclosure about the foundation to the buyers. Potential crisis finally averted, they had it fully repaired before moving in. Had they not done so, the long-term stability of the structure would likely have been compromised.

A house's foundation is critical. No matter how nice the home looks, no matter what features it has, if its foundation is unstable, it's only a matter of time before it begins to crumble.

A sad reality is that even when a home has a weak foundation, the tendency is to ignore the problem. That's what we did in our house. After all, until it gets really bad, no one can really see the negative effects, right? So the typical homeowner decorates and landscapes and details the house, making everything look wonderful on the surface. But all the while, the home is slowly falling apart.

The Nonnegotiable Foundation of a Parent's Walk with God

In our discipleship paradigm, *abiding*—or a parent's personal relationship with God—is the foundation we choose to build on. And it's the very thing parents tend to neglect the most.

As parents, we typically spend a great deal of time working on what others can see, making sure those around us know we're

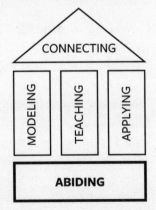

good moms and dads. We do everything we can to provide all the things accepted as necessary for a happy childhood: a nice house, material possessions, fashionable clothes, involvement in all the right activities, vacations to all the right places. We want everyone to notice that our kids are getting everything they need to grow up happy.

The reality is that what our kids need most is a parent who walks intimately with God. Everything hinges on this one aspect that's so essential yet so easily overlooked. Our tendency is to downplay its importance because it's part of our private lives and not easily seen. Nobody readily knows if we're talking to Jesus, clinging to Him, reading His Word, or listening for His voice. Nonetheless, our ability to effectively parent our children is critically dependent on remaining intimate with Christ.

What our kids need most is a parent who walks intimately with God.

As I shared in the last chapter, in John 15:5 Jesus made one thing clear when He said, "I am the vine, you are the branches; the one who remains in Me, and I in him bears much fruit, for apart from Me you can do nothing" (NASB). Just as a branch has to stay connected to its vine in order to be useful, staying connected to God is critical for the Christ-follower. Jesus refers to this connection as *abiding*. When we fail to abide in Him, we can't expect to accomplish anything of lasting value.

Still, many well-meaning and highly motivated parents diligently strive to raise their kids to "turn out right" only

58

to find themselves frustrated and failing. Their kids aren't interested in the things of God and might even totally reject the values they've so diligently poured into them.

If you're a parent in this situation and you're searching for answers, the first place to look is your own walk with Christ. It's possible that you've been trusting in your own hard work and discipline to such an extent that you've failed to stay "connected to the vine"—forgoing this most important command in exchange for greater effort on your part.

In our ministry to parents, we encounter far too many moms and dads working a checklist of what they think good parents should be doing. They treat their role as a Christian parent as an if-then formula: *If I do these things, then my children will love and follow Jesus.* While certainly the Christian life has best practices, no guaranteed formulas exist. Walking with Christ is far more valuable to our souls than working our checklists.

We're all prone to forget this. We forget that God created us to be human beings and instead turn into human doings. Our culture has convinced us that the solution to any shortcoming or failure is to try harder—to do more. But Jesus taught a completely different way.

In his simple yet powerful book *Secrets of the Vine*, Bruce Wilkinson notes:

Within six verses in John 15, Jesus says *abide* ten times. You can sense the passion and poignancy of His plea. Jesus knows that He is about to leave His friends, yet He is saying, "We must be together." He knows that in the coming years, these downcast, frightened men now standing with Him in the vineyard will be called to produce an unheard-of, miraculous amount of fruit—enough fruit to turn the whole world upside down.

And Jesus knows they can't begin to achieve that kind of eternal impact without the one thing they're most likely to forget: more of Him.[2]

Limited vs. Unlimited Power

I have a clear memory of when Hurricane Alicia rolled through South Texas in the fall of 1983, taking most of Houston's electrical infrastructure with it. The storm decimated much of the city and left numerous homes without power for as many as ten days. In my family's case, we went a full week without it. As a fairly bright teenager, I knew the air conditioner, lights, and electrical appliances in our home wouldn't work until power was restored. Still, I found myself doing the same idiotic thing over and over again: I kept trying to turn things on.

Every time I walked into a dark room, I flipped the light switch. I'd grab the TV remote and push the power button. I'd be thirsty and check the refrigerator for a cold drink. And every single time, for a brief moment I was sure that whatever the thing, it would work. Of course, I'd kick myself for being so boneheaded. But then not five minutes later I'd walk into another room and do it again. Call me a creature of habit.

How many times do we do the exact same thing, over and over, trying to accomplish what God has called us to do, all while neglecting the power found only in our relationship with Him? Even though it's consistently fruitless, we keep doing it the same way, trying even harder, wearing ourselves out all the more. The problem is not a lack of ability or commitment but that we're not plugged into our power source.

While a few Christian parents might find themselves fully isolated from any form of spiritual power, the majority of us fall into the trap of settling for what's potentially more dangerous: living on temporary, limited power.

In the middle of that disastrous week when we had no electricity, my dad got his hands on a portable generator. He filled the tank with gas, put it in our driveway, and then hard-wired it directly into our home's service panel. Immediately, we had power all through the house. But while this was a definite improvement, the power was limited. It was just enough to keep the fridge going and to turn on a few lights and fans. But too many things running at once would shut down the generator. We liked having power, but we could do only so much with this effective yet limited source.

In the same way, I like going to church, and I like being with God's people. I enjoy worship and the teaching of the Word. Like many believers, I get home on Sunday afternoon feeling encouraged, filled, and focused on Christ. I confess that sometimes I also feel like what I get in those few hours on Sunday will take me through the rest of the week. Add to that a midweek Bible study or prayer group, and I think I have all I need to sustain my spiritual health.

What a perfectly subtle lie the enemy has me believing! He has me trusting in limited power. He has me happily settling for a portable generator when God is offering me a connection to the power grid. The enemy knows that when the temporary power of my Sunday visit to church runs out, my only choice is to fall back on my flesh. And my flesh will have just enough spiritual understanding to successfully deceive my heart into thinking I'm doing things God's way.

Perhaps the only thing more dangerous than living life in the flesh is living it in the flesh while thinking I'm walking in the Spirit.

Paul warned Timothy that this type of pseudo-Christian living would be rampant in the coming days:

> But mark this: There will be terrible times in the last days. People will be lovers of themselves, lovers of money, boastful, proud, abusive, disobedient to their parents, ungrateful, unholy, without love, unforgiving, slanderous, without self-control, brutal, not lovers of the good, treacherous, rash, conceited, lovers of pleasure rather than lovers of God—*having a form of godliness but denying its power.*
>
> 2 Timothy 3:1–5 (emphasis mine)

While we may not see ourselves in this list of ungodly behaviors, we probably know what it feels like to attempt to live a godly life yet still feel powerless. This can easily happen when we exchange abiding in Christ for something much more convenient, such as church attendance. But Jesus doesn't want us to simply accept the spoon-feeding of knowledge from a pastor or Bible study teacher. He wants us to join Him at a buffet table where He can personally pour Himself and His truth into us.

Abiding in Christ Is What You Were Made For

While abiding has a foundational place in our discipleship paradigm for parents, I'm not suggesting that our motivation for intimacy with God is for our kids to turn out right. Far more is at stake here. We stay close to Christ not so we can get the results we want but because it's the core purpose of our lives.

> *We stay close to Christ not so we can get the results we want but because it's the core purpose of our lives.*

God created Adam—and you and me—purely for His own pleasure. He desires fellowship with people to whom He's given free will and who will voluntarily choose to worship Him. I like the simple way Paul puts it: "God is faithful, who has called you into fellowship with his Son, Jesus Christ our Lord" (1 Corinthians 1:9).

When we live in fellowship with Jesus—talking to Him, listening to Him, and sharing our days with Him—the result is that we bear fruit. Good things naturally come out of us when we're a healthy branch connected to a powerful vine. When we place the highest priority on staying connected to Jesus instead of on being a good parent, we give God the opportunity to supernaturally transform us into both the people and parents He's called us to be.

The Result of a Missing Foundation

When a house is missing its foundation, the entire structure is compromised. In a similar way, your best intentions for discipleship with your kids will crumble because you can do nothing of real spiritual value if the foundation of abiding is missing from your life.

When we try to live without staying closely connected to Jesus, He makes it clear that we can do "nothing"—*not a thing*. And when it comes to parenting our kids, the same holds true. Sure, we can successfully help them do well in school, excel in extracurricular activities, and develop satisfying friendships. We can do all that and more without abiding in Christ.

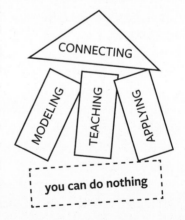

But that's not our objective. Remember, our God-given objective is to make disciples.

Jesus tells us we will bear much fruit when we abide in Him, and the opposite is also true. Just as you can't expect grapes from a branch that's been severed from the vine, you can't bear any fruit as a parent if you're disconnected from Jesus. You can raise "good kids," but you can't make disciples.

Jesus did all He did so His disciples could duplicate what He'd done and continue with His ministry once He was physically gone. In the same way, we want our kids to be able to bear fruit long after we're removed from their daily lives. No amount of hard work and goal setting will produce any lasting fruit if we're living apart from Christ. The process of spiritual growth in us and in our kids is entirely supernatural. It has nothing to do with us and everything to do with the power of God. That's why abiding in Christ is so essential.

How to Start Building Intimacy with God

Building intimacy with God isn't easy. If we already know parenting is hard work, then we can expect that building a foundation for our parenting paradigm will be challenging. Still, it's the essential command God gives us.

Again quoting Bruce Wilkinson, "*Abide* is an imperative—not a suggestion or request. You don't have to command a child to eat dessert. You command someone to do something because it's not going to come naturally."[3]

A REAL-LIFE PARENTING STORY

Listening to the Voice of God

Tina and Ron were faithful Christians raising two daughters. They loved their girls, but Tina honestly didn't know what to do with these two little people God had entrusted to her. The family stayed busy with school, church, and life, but she desperately wanted purpose as she parented.

When Tina studied her Bible, she was amazed at how often the characters there heard God's voice. They received clear instructions from a God who was both close and clear on His instructions. When she started to realize that He wanted to lead her and tell her what to do as well, Tina turned her prayer life into more of a conversation. After bringing her requests, she asked questions and then made a point of being quiet so she could listen for the "still, small voice" of God.

Today Tina says she doesn't hear a loud, booming voice. Instead, God impresses what she should be doing with her girls on her heart. She gets insight from Him regarding what's at the root of their behavior and attitudes. Most importantly, as she walks in a relationship with God, He fills her heart with purpose. She feels His power and presence moving through her every day.

This is the joy found in staying close to the Father.

If walking in fellowship with God doesn't come naturally to us, then we can take disciplined steps to make it possible. And though there's no set formula for accomplishing this, let me offer the following four suggestions as a starting place.

1. Begin at the Beginning

Start by confirming that you are in fact a follower of Jesus Christ. Jesus gave the command to abide to those who had already committed their lives to Him. If you haven't professed faith in Christ and given Him control of your life, then it's impossible to find the strength and power that come from being with Him. You still have a sin problem that separates you from God. The requirement for you is simple: "Repent, then, and turn to God, so that your sins may be wiped out, that times of refreshing may come from the Lord" (Acts 3:19).

I like the way Peter described salvation in his sermon in Acts 3. As you repent of your sin and your rebellion against God, you're returning to what you were made to be. You're discovering God's original plan for your life: to know Him and be with Him.

If you have questions about salvation or want assurance of your relationship with Christ, I encourage you to speak with a trusted Christian friend, pastor, or someone else who can give you wise counsel. You'll want to get this nailed down if you hope to bear any lasting fruit as you parent your children.

2. Focus on Your Relationship with God

Another key is regularly asking God to help you fall more deeply in love with Him. In the book of Revelation, John recorded Christ's words to the church at Ephesus, where He affirmed their hard work but reminded them that they were still missing the point:

> I know your deeds, your hard work and your perseverance. I know that you cannot tolerate wicked people, that you have tested those who claim to be apostles but are not, and have found them false. You have persevered and have endured hardships for my name, and have not grown weary. Yet I hold this against you: You have forsaken the love you had at first.
>
> Revelation 2:2–4

How many of us in the church today have replaced simple devotion to Christ with busy activity done in His name? But the calling on every believer's life is to nurture and maintain a passionate love for Christ, our first love. Begin to see Him as the friend who's always right beside you and loves you like no other. In a world where so many people and relationships are vying for our affection, we can daily ask God to birth in our hearts a focused love for and commitment to Him.

3. Stop Depending on Your Hard Work

Another key step is to admit that you're nothing without Jesus, that your efforts are meaningless. Even striving to abide in Christ can become a fleshly pursuit, especially for "movers and shakers." While spiritual disciplines are certainly of great value, you can't trust in your diligence as the means to a deeper life in Christ. Instead, ask God to supernaturally do in you what you can't do on your own. Admit that you aren't strong enough, smart enough, or committed enough to pursue Him like you want to. In confessing your inability, you're paving the way for God to get to work in your life.

Paul wrote, "[Christ] said to me, 'My grace is sufficient for you, for my power is made perfect in weakness.' Therefore I will boast all the more gladly about my weaknesses, so that Christ's power may rest on me" (2 Corinthians 12:9). Paul rightly realized that his weakness was a good thing, mainly because it forced him and his flesh out of the way. After all, this is a spiritual pursuit that transcends all our human understanding of hard work and achievement. Confessing that we can't abide in Christ without His help is essential.

4. Remember That God is Always with You

Finally, begin making all this possible by developing a keen awareness of and sensitivity to the moment-by-moment presence of God in your life. Seventeenth-century monk Brother Lawrence referred to this as "practicing the presence of Christ."[4]

An excellent spiritual exercise is to imagine what your daily life would be like if Jesus were physically present with you. Imagine how you would speak, handle temptation, and share

your faith if He were by your side. I like to think I'd be an absolute spiritual powerhouse if Jesus were right here with me.
After all, Jesus would be watching me (and I want to please
Him) and encouraging me (He would have my back wherever
I went). So I would use only words that were a blessing to others. I would stand tall in the face of even the most overwhelming of temptations. I would witness to anything that breathed.

Yes, if Jesus were physically present, then abiding would
be much easier.

While this might seem like wishful thinking, the truth is
Christ's continual presence is a reality for all Christians. We
must remember that God has given us His Holy Spirit, the
very presence of God residing in the life of every believer. We
actively choose to believe that Jesus was telling the truth
when He said, "Surely I am with you always, to the very end
of the age" (Matthew 28:20).

Jesus is always with you. Let those words sink in. Recognize
that you don't go anywhere that Jesus doesn't go with you.
You don't do anything that He doesn't see. You don't have any
thought that He doesn't know. See this as a very good thing—
a reality that truly enables abiding in Him to be a possibility
for every believer, including you.

Ask God to Search Your Heart and Mind

As this chapter comes to a close, I invite you to spend a
few minutes in personal introspection (yes, even before

you arrive at the "For Personal Reflection" section at the end). Speak to God about your personal relationship with Him. Ask Him to search the deepest parts of your heart and mind—the parts nobody sees—to discover how much you're trusting in Him and to what extent you're depending on yourself.

Perhaps you could pray a prayer like David prayed: "Search me, God, and know my heart; test me and know my anxious thoughts. See if there is any offensive way in me, and lead me in the way everlasting" (Psalm 139:23–24). When you give God permission to search the depths of your heart and you're willing to face whatever He brings to the surface, it isn't always a pleasurable experience. While He'll brag about how proud He is of all that we are, He'll also point out where we're falling short.

The great thing is that He meets us there, loves us despite our shortcomings, and welcomes us into deeper fellowship with Him. And each and every time we invite God to look a little bit deeper, He has the opportunity to stretch our faith and we have the opportunity to savor the joy of a deeper surrender to Him.

If you're willing to invite God to search your heart, be sincerely open to three possible responses from Him:

He helps you face the hard truth that you've never given your life to Christ and have no idea what it really means to be a Christian. Know you're in a truly

71

wonderful place. Listen closely as He quietly whispers your name, inviting you into salvation from your sin and a personal relationship with Him, the God of all creation.

He confronts you with the reality that you've been neglecting your relationship with Him. Simply return to your first love. What a thrill it will be to fall in love again! He welcomes you back with no condemnation and no lectures. Like the father who saw his prodigal son coming down the road, God runs to welcome you back with open arms.

He shows you that many of the accomplishments and successes the world has bestowed on you as a parent are meaningless in His kingdom. Accept this truth with humility. Then listen as God begins to reveal what truly matters to Him in your life and in your family. He offers you Himself as the ultimate resource to bear fruit that lasts in your home and with your kids.

If you feel you're in any way not connected to Christ like you want to be, then put this book aside and do whatever it takes to get there. Don't pick it up again until you've found an essential, satisfying, and dependent relationship with Jesus. It will be impossible for God to build the rest of this house of discipleship in your home until the foundation is established.

Here's the good news: once you begin to abide in Christ as He commands, there's no end to the miraculous and lasting things God can build both in you and in the generations that will follow after you.

FOR PERSONAL Reflection

- Read John 15:5 again. (This is a great verse to commit to memory.)
- Why is it so important for you to abide or remain in Christ as you disciple your children? How does parenting go for you when you neglect your relationship with Him—when you're not praying or in the Word?
- What are two or three ways you can diligently abide in Christ in your daily life at home? Perhaps by beginning your day with a prayer asking God to remind you of His presence in your life today. Or maybe by carving out moments of silence where you invite God to speak to you about your needs and the needs of your kids.
- Ask God to give you a greater desire to be close to Him. If you don't have a real thirst for the things of Jesus, ask Him to supernaturally birth it in you. That's the type of prayer He loves to say yes to!

MODELING

Living an Authentic Christian Life

Don't worry that your children never listen to you; worry that they are always watching you.

—*Robert Fulghum*

When I became a first-time father three long decades ago (practically the Stone Age), I knew my role would be significant in raising this new baby and providing for her needs. But I was just coming into an understanding of the importance of my own character and life in laying the framework for her growth and development.

Then one afternoon, there I was, minding my own business, unaware that God was about to make it real clear for me. While listening to Christian radio, I heard a song that succinctly captured the essence of my responsibility over the next twenty years or so. Phillips, Craig & Dean—each singing in the role of a Christian parent—offered a lyric that conveyed their desperate desire to be just like Jesus. Why? Because their child wanted to be just like them.[1]

From that moment on I knew my personal commitment to becoming more like Christ would be vitally important to the spiritual growth of all my children. What they saw in me would most likely be naturally integrated into their own lives.

Our Kids Need a Good Role Model

Let's consider again our discipleship paradigm. If abiding in Christ becomes a regular part of our lives, then the most natural by-product will be an authentic, Spirit-filled life. This is where the Christian parent builds the first essential pillar in the process of discipling their child: *modeling*. We can all be sure that more is caught than taught.

Pastor and author Kevin DeYoung put it this way: "The one indispensable requirement for producing godly, mature Christians is godly, mature Christians."[2] Because of this reality, we can live and demonstrate the Christian life long before we begin the process of teaching it to our kids. This is the reason modeling is one of three essential pillars in our paradigm.

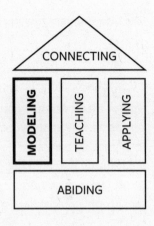

When we consider Jesus and His disciples, we can be confident that He never asked anything of them they'd not already seen Him model in the normal practice of His life and ministry. Christ certainly understood that the best way to teach for impact was to provide a clear model for others to emulate.

Jesus' discipleship style was radically different from the legalistic realities His followers were used to. Instead of giving them a long list of requirements and to-do lists, as did the religious leaders of the day, He offered His very life as an example. In many ways He told them, "You can know the ways of God by watching Me. Love like I love. Speak like I speak. Pray like I pray. If you're confused about the priorities and values of your heavenly Father, watch My life and learn."

What must it have been like for those twelve chosen disciples to be granted what was often 24/7 access to our Lord? They could grow every single day in their understanding of what God was actually like by watching the Son, Jesus, doing everyday life before their eyes.

The Life-Changing Power of an Example

If someone asked you to name the most powerful and essential scriptural truth for parents, what Bible verse or verses would you choose? What if you had to identify a single passage of Scripture that would serve as your key principle for raising and discipling your kids?

My favorite passage on this is not commonly known as a parenting guide. In fact, tucked away in a nearly hidden little place in Exodus 33, it's one of those portions of Scripture most people probably pass right over, missing the powerful truth it contains.

The context is that Moses has led the children of Israel out of captivity in Egypt and into the desert through the Red Sea. God has miraculously delivered them from Pharaoh, given them His law, and instructed them to build a tabernacle to worship Him. Yet even though they've seen numerous signs and wonders, the people still waver in their commitment to God. Their most recent rebellion was to build a golden calf to worship.

As leader and primary mediator with God, Moses needed to stay close to the Father, and here a typical encounter between the two of them is described:

> Now Moses used to take the tent and pitch it outside the camp, a good distance from the camp, and he called it the tent of meeting. And everyone who sought the LORD would go out

78

to the tent of meeting which was outside the camp. And it came about, whenever Moses went out to the tent, that all the people would arise and stand, each at the entrance of his tent, and gaze after Moses until he entered the tent. Whenever Moses entered the tent, the pillar of cloud would descend and stand at the entrance of the tent; and the LORD would speak with Moses. When all the people saw the pillar of cloud standing at the entrance of the tent, all the people would stand and worship, each at the entrance of his tent. So the LORD used to speak to Moses face to face, just as a man speaks to his friend. When Moses returned to the camp, his servant Joshua, the son of Nun, a young man, would not depart from the tent.

Exodus 33:7–11 NASB

Let me summarize what you just read:

- First, Moses would meet with God in the tent.
- Second, God would show up in obvious ways.
- Third, the people would know God was there as evidenced by the pillar of cloud that showed up.
- Fourth, God would speak to Moses in a way that was personal and real. At this time in history, only Moses had this type of relationship with Him.
- Finally (and this is the part I don't want you to miss), when Moses would finish meeting with God and return to the camp, his young assistant Joshua would not leave the tent.

The big question is why Joshua wouldn't leave the tent. Maybe he stuck around to clean up after Moses because his boss was messy. But I think something more significant was happening. I believe he wouldn't leave because of what he regularly saw happen between Moses and God.

This passage suggests there was more at work in Joshua's maturation process than good teaching on Moses' part. Something powerful was being passed on in the form of a compelling example. Moses' relationship with God and the life he modeled before Joshua was absolutely magnetic. While Scripture doesn't specifically say this, I believe that when Moses' time with God was over, Joshua stuck around, lingering in the wake of the presence of God, because he was looking for leftovers.

Joshua saw up close what Moses experienced with God. While the rest of the Israelites saw it from afar, he had a front-row seat to a real, authentic, life-changing relationship with the Father. He saw what Moses had, and he wanted it too.

Do you see the application to your role as a parent? While most every Christian mom or dad seeks ways to get their children more interested in the things of God, few start by looking in the right place: the mirror. They evaluate their kids' Sunday school class, scrutinize their peers, and make sure they're protected from the evils of TikTok, but the greatest single factor in developing a child's interest in God is their parents' example. They need to see in Mom and Dad that Jesus is worth following.

Every children's pastor, Sunday school teacher, and student minister they've ever had has told them that walking in a daily relationship with God is the key to a meaningful life. The problem is they can find so few people who are experiencing that life. As in the words of the classic U2 song, most teenagers would confess they still haven't found what they're looking for.[3] The sad thing is that they find very little evidence that the Christian adults around them have found it either.

And that includes their parents.

The greatest single factor in developing a child's interest in God is their parents' example. They need to see in Mom and Dad that Jesus is worth following.

George Barna, perhaps the most credible researcher in the Christian community, has suggested that today's young people are the most spiritually inclined generation in decades. They're searching for meaning in the sacred things of life, desiring a spiritual revelation of God and a true life-changing connection to a community of faith. They desire a relevant belief system that impacts their lives. The bad news is that the first and primary place they look for meaningful faith is in their parents. Yet Barna's research suggests they're having a hard time finding it.[4]

As a mother or father, you are the clearest picture of the Christian life your kids will ever see. They're not turning into their student minister or Bible study teacher. In the grand scope of things, they're turning into you. It's unreasonable (and even silly) to assume that involving your kids in a church program for one or more hours each week will result in their developing into fully devoted followers of Christ, especially if they're not seeing that life modeled at home.

The Messages Your Children Ignore and the One They Hear

In their book *Guiding Your Teen to a Faith That Lasts*, authors Kevin Huggins and Phil Landrum share this telling observation: we often—even constantly—give our children messages in an effort to teach and lead them toward sound beliefs, character, and behavior, but that doesn't mean they actually hear them. And they give us some particularly ineffective messages kids can get from their parents on a regular basis:

- Kids ignore the "*conflicting messages*" parents give when they don't see actions backing up words. It's even worse when they see their parents saying one thing and then doing the exact opposite.
- Kids tune out "*angry messages*" delivered by parents. While a parent may think the only time their kid listens to them is when they get loud, the opposite is true. They are actually tuning us out, waiting for the anger to subside.
- Kids don't listen to "*extraneous messages*" that don't seem relevant to their situation. While parents may think they are addressing the issues their kids are dealing with, many times we don't take enough time to listen to accurately address what they are facing.[5]

But then Huggins and Landrum go on to say that one message parents give their kids is the one the kids hear the loudest and clearest. Unbeknownst to you, it's constantly being communicated to them, picked up in thousands of unspoken and unintended ways through the natural, daily activity of your life.

What speaks loudest and clearest to your children is your passion.[6]

Whatever has the greatest value to you will inevitably spill out to your children. And they'll tend to learn that it should be important to them as well. Your passion and devotion will be broadcast loudly to your kids by the daily choices you make, what you talk about and spend money on, and will usually drown out all the other messages you're trying to communicate.

To test this premise, a few years ago I conducted a simple experiment with the teenagers at my church. I asked them this simple question: "What are your parents passionate about?" Consider these somewhat bleak yet typical responses:

"Mom is passionate about buying stuff to make our lives better."

"Dad's is golf. He plays every Sunday, but if he can't, he watches it on TV."

"Dad is passionate about his job. It's his dream to be what he is and more. It's very important to him."

83

"Mom's passion is for me to always look and dress neat
... at church, at school, wherever I go."

"Dad is passionate about the stock market and anything
that has to do with making money."

"Mom wants me to be popular."

"Dad's passion is football. He never misses one of my
games."

I received a few encouraging responses, though. Answers
like:

"Mom's passion is making sure we know how to keep
God number one."

"Dad's passion is sharing his faith with others."

"Both my parents are very passionate about living for
the Lord because they're always talking about Him to
each other and to us."

Those authors' theory held true in the families of those
teens in my church. While I recognize that only God can
judge the heart, I can say that those kids who described their
parents' passions in terms of material desires and temporary
goals were generally immature Christians characterized by
self-centered lives. Those who characterized their parents
as devoted to Christ were kids who led Christlike lives as
well.

It's the "God to Moses to Joshua" principle from Exodus 33 at work. And it's what Paul tried to do in his letter to the church when he wrote, "Follow my example."

The best and clearest way to grow young Christians into mature Christians is to give them someone to model. Someone who conveys, *Do you want to know how to pray? Pray like me. How to serve? Serve like I do. How to love people? Watch how I love people.* Fundamentally, parents must strive to be what they want their kids to be.

When a Clear Model Is Absent

Consider our discipling paradigm again. I know that in chapter 2 I said it doesn't work to master one component of this model and then move on to another. But if you try to move into the essential components of teaching and applying without out first modeling the life you want your children to embrace, you're sending a contradictory message that even the youngest child can and will pick up on. A lifestyle marked by this type of behavior is known as *hypocrisy*, which makes us the worst kind of teacher/discipler.

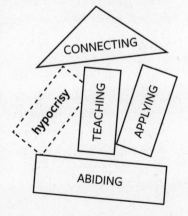

85

If you're not serving as an effective model and your life hints of hypocrisy, it's likely to have the same impact on your parenting that termites can have on a house. While you might not notice the effects at first, slowly but surely the strength of the house is being compromised. It's only a matter of time before it begins to crumble from within. Even if you're teaching your kids with diligence and helping them apply truth to their lives, you won't be able to help them build a solid, lasting faith if you're not modeling the life you're leading them into.

At best, this contradictory lifestyle will be copied by your children. They'll learn to say one thing and do another, to live a marginal faith that makes little difference in daily life. At worst, they'll reject your faith altogether if they don't see it working in your own Christian walk.

Jesus gave a stern warning to His disciples about the perils of following the Pharisees, textbook-case hypocrites whose walk didn't match their talk:

> The teachers of the law and the Pharisees sit in Moses' seat. So you must be careful to do everything they tell you. But do not do what they do, for they do not practice what they preach. They tie up heavy, cumbersome loads and put them on other people's shoulders, but they themselves are not willing to lift a finger to move them.

Matthew 23:2–4

Jesus instructs His followers to obey good instruction but ignore the lifestyle of the one doing the teaching, a difficult undertaking at best. One of the hardest things for any of us to do is follow someone who's not providing a good example. Perhaps this is why Jesus describes the Pharisees as ones who "tie up heavy, cumbersome loads and put them on other people's shoulders" (verse 4).

What if this stern warning is directed to our children in reference to us? What if we're the Pharisees? How difficult is it for our kids to follow Christ's teachings if we're living lifestyles contradictory to what we're encouraging or even demanding from our kids? If they see the Christian faith as a "heavy burden," could it be they're seeing inconsistent, hypocritical behavior on our part?

> *Talk is cheap. We can say we're committed to Christ, but our lives will honestly reflect whether our faith is authentic.*

Talk is cheap. We can say we're committed to Christ, but our lives will honestly reflect whether our faith is authentic. And our children will watch us, picking up cues. They'll either learn how to devote their lives fully to Christ or learn how to be a hypocrite. And they'll learn this best from their parents. This is why modeling is so important.

A REAL-LIFE PARENTING STORY

They Do What We Do

Many years ago my son had just turned the corner in learning to read, and I encouraged him to spend some time in his Bible each day. But I was soon frustrated because he didn't seem particularly interested. Even my most passionate pleas didn't seem to motivate him.

A couple of months later, God showed me what was missing. As a pastor, I had the privilege of working in an office environment where personal Bible study and prayer were encouraged. So I typically found it easier to have my personal devotion times there. While that was certainly a blessing, God pointed out that my son rarely saw me in the Word. How could I expect from my child what he didn't clearly see as important in my own life?

While I continued to take advantage of my office hours for study, I began doing Bible readings as part of my daily routine at home. Within a few weeks, I noticed my son was reading his Bible every night before going to bed, all without my saying another word to him.

Modeling desired behavior speaks so much louder than can ever be communicated with lofty speeches or compelling arguments.

Practical Ways to Jump-Start Your Modeling Career

What if you're not sure how you're doing in the modeling department? Consider the following four practical steps as a starting place to becoming the example your kids so desperately need.

1. Take a Look in the Mirror

Perhaps now would be a great time to set this book aside, take a nice long look at yourself, and prayerfully ask yourself the following questions:

- *What are my habits, sins, and weaknesses that don't honor God?* (You might want to ask God this question too.)
- *What tendencies or priorities have I inherited from generations before me that I'm committed to halting before they settle into my kids' lives?*
- *What are the disciplines, behaviors, and values I want my children to embrace, and do they see them lived out in my life?*

If God reveals things that need to change or be adjusted, then I can assure you He wants to help you change them. Accept the forgiveness He offers and move forward in His grace and strength.

Next, before God and in the presence of your spouse or a trusted Christian friend, you can make a vow to seek their help in making the changes that need to take place. Remember, the legacy you'll pass on to many generations is at stake.

2. Allow Christ to Be Obvious in Your Life

The Christian faith is all about a relationship with God, which too many people never truly figure out. And if you don't share this reality of Christ in your life with your kids, it's unlikely they'll embrace an intimate relationship with Him for themselves. Yes, they might acknowledge Christianity as a belief system or an organized set of rules, but that's all.

The Christian parents who desire their children to love Christ will clearly model a love relationship with Him. So be willing, when appropriate, to wear your faith on your sleeve. When Christ speaks to you, teaches you something, or uses you somehow, share it with your kids. Let them know that God is alive and well in your life.

3. Start Practicing What You Preach—Before You Preach It

Consider the behaviors, beliefs, and convictions you want your kids to develop and ultimately put into practice. Make a list of them and then ask yourself, *Do my kids regularly see me model these?* If the answer is no, then stop wasting your time trying to teach them.

Instead, ask God for a season of time when you can begin practicing the things you know are the most valuable in life. Pray for a renewed hunger for His Word and a desire to meet with Him in fellowship and prayer. Then as these disciplines become a natural part of your life, let your children catch you praying, studying, witnessing, and so on.

The habits of prayer, Bible study, Scripture memory, meditation, silence, and others can serve an invaluable function in our daily walk with Christ. Don't, however, practice them as public displays in an effort to train your children but as a means to draw near to Christ, the One who's always there for us yet our flesh tends to ignore.

This leads me to the fourth and final place to start:

4. Make Christ Your Sincere Passion, and Then Live a Passionate Life

Again, remember that of all the messages we send our kids, our passion is the one they hear the loudest and clearest. And it's impossible to fake this one. Either you have a passionate commitment to Christ and His ways or you don't. Your life is devoted to building God's kingdom or to building your own. Anyone who knows you well can tell which one is the commitment of your heart. They can see where you invest your time, your treasure, and your very life. And while you might be able to fool others, your kids know your true heart better than just about anyone.

They need to see a parent who:

- is passionately in love with Christ
- walks daily with Him
- often talks about Him and His activity
- listens to His voice
- serves Him with gladness
- obeys Him with sincerity and pleasure
- gives to Him generously and often
- rearranges their schedule to make room for Him—lots of Him
- worships Him with unspeakable joy!

Do all those things you naturally do when you're deeply in love with and grateful to God. Do them not as acts performed in front of your kids but as the natural outpouring of who you are. Rest assured that your kids will notice. They'll be impacted so much more by who you are than by what you say. Because the reality remains that your children are turning into *you*.

They grow up so fast, and our time with them is so short. Your children need an authentic Christian model right now! Ask God to reveal any things in your life clouding your child's impression of who Jesus is and what it means to be His disciple. Then look to Him for the power to change and adjust toward a God-centered life. As He does, watch with anticipation for the amazing things He'll do both in your life and the lives of your children.

FOR PERSONAL
Reflection

- Read Philippians 4:9.
- Why is it so important for you to lead by example as you disciple your children? How do you see your children following others?
- What are two or three things you can do this week to be a better model of Christian living for your kids? For example, let your kids catch you praying or studying Scripture.
- If you asked your children what your passions are, what would they say? (Maybe actually ask them.) If it's not first and foremost your love for Jesus and His work, then what needs to change?
- Ask God to show you how to be a better model of the Christian life for your kids to watch and copy every day.

TEACHING

Pointing Your Children to the Truth

Let no Christian parents fall into the delusion that Sunday-school is intended to ease them of their personal duties. The first and most natural condition of things is for Christian parents to train up their own children in the nurture and admonition of the Lord.

—*Charles Spurgeon*[1]

I did a lot of spectacularly stupid things as a young teenager. I thought a lot of foolish thoughts. I had some terrible ideas of how the world worked. And one thing I believed shows how absolutely idiotic I could be.

When I was in the early years of middle school and hadn't taken the time to adequately prepare for a test, I would sleep with the book or class notes under my pillow. I thought the knowledge they held would somehow be transferred directly to my brain as I slept. I called it the "osmosis method," based on the scientific principle that water can transfer from one cell to another when their pressure and proximity are right. Surely, I reasoned, keeping the information and the pressure I was under close by would cause me to learn what I needed to know.

While my preadolescent belief in this utter foolishness proves that kids can be dumber than dirt, I confess that I've carried some form of this thinking into my adulthood. Specifically, I can tend to believe that my kids will learn about God and following Jesus simply because they're around me. Somehow what I believe and hold dear will automatically—through osmosis—be embraced by my children.

While modeling is essential, at some point I need to actually open my mouth (and my Bible) to articulate the hows, whys, and ways of God to them.

Your Kids Need You to Teach Them

Yes, your kids will pick up on what you live out in front of them. That's why setting an example and giving them a life to emulate is one of the three main pillars of our discipleship model. It is, however, only one of the three. At some point there has to be more, and that's where *teaching* comes in.

As a parent committed to making disciples in your home, you'll want to teach your kids why your family believes what it believes. And you'll want to do it in a way that enables them to embrace it as truth for their own lives despite what the world tells them.

Our discipleship model continues to follow the example of what Jesus did with His disciples. Of all the things He did with the Twelve, teaching stands out as fundamental. As a rabbi (teacher) He was constantly communicating what it looked like to live as part of God's kingdom here on earth.

Sure, He was modeling it for those closest to Him, but that wasn't enough. In their first-century world dominated by the cultural norms of both their Hebrew tradition and Roman occupation, He needed to confront wrong ways of thinking and replace them with truth. Absent that, Jesus' disciples never would have truly learned how God intended the world to work. The influence of their environment was way too strong.

If that held true two thousand years ago, then it certainly holds true in our world today. And at levels that are absolutely unprecedented. Think about it:

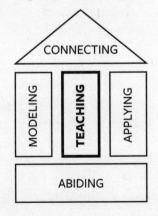

In every single generation before ours, parents were able to teach their kids the worldview of their choosing. They could raise their children to embrace whatever values and beliefs the family embraced, all with some measure of insulation from opposing viewpoints. Sure, young people would hear and consider other perspectives they encountered at school or out in the world somewhere, but those interactions were limited. By and large, the parents—and the community they chose—had the greatest influence. By a wide margin.

Fast-forward to our smartphone generation. The digital natives we're raising in our homes today have access—via the unfettered availability of technology—to every worldview on the planet. They're exposed to a greater influx of opposing perspectives than any generation in history. The social media platforms our kids flock to give voice and legitimacy to the most demented and twisted belief systems imaginable.

Sadly, our children don't have to go looking for any of this. These popular apps intentionally push content their way. Then the algorithms work behind the scenes to give them more and more of it once they click on whatever topic or subject is popular at the time. The net result is a bombardment of information from cool, smart, and seemingly authoritative influencers whose perspectives go unchallenged in a world where all perspectives are valid. It's no wonder young people are walking away from the faith in record numbers.

If parents aren't intentionally teaching the truth, then we can assume their kids are buying into lies. And if they're spending a lot of time on social media, then it's a foregone conclusion. I can hear what you're thinking: *We take our kids to church!* I hate to say this—although I do several times in this book—but that's not nearly enough. Your kids' church attendance isn't making a dent in this problem. Not a dent.

The Babylon Bee satirical platform captured this perfectly in a hilarious article. The post has a picture of a concerned mom watching her teenage son looking at his smartphone, and the headline reads, "Parents baffled that 1 hour of youth group a week not effectively combating teen's 30 hours on TikTok."[2] Millions of Christian parents are equally baffled.

Just as the twelve disciples needed Jesus to teach them about God's kingdom, it's up to parents to teach the next generation the ways of Jesus. God has entrusted you and you alone with this role. Proverbs 22:6 commands us, "Train up a child in the way he should go, even when he grows older he will not abandon it" (NASB).

As parents, we can cling to this promise of hope only if we intentionally do the training it entails. The church might help, and the community we live in can reinforce truth, but the home is the primary place where learning happens. That means parents get to be teachers. And if you have any takeaway from reading these words, my hope is that you ultimately feel the burden of responsibility for your children's Christian education and spiritual development.

Teaching like Jesus doesn't mean we train our Christian kids to get along in the larger society. It's just the opposite.

Too many people of faith have settled for a watered-down version of Christianity where their faith makes them nice people with success in the world. But we have a far higher calling than being nice and successful. Jesus' invitation to be His disciples means we take up our cross and follow Him. This requires self-sacrifice and a rejection of the world's ideas of success.

Parents who want their kids to be fully successful in God's eyes and at the same time fully successful in the world's eyes usually fail at both.

Parents who want their kids to be fully successful in God's eyes and at the same time fully successful in the world's eyes usually fail at both. Christian parenting requires that we choose God's value system over what the world has to offer.

If you haven't thought about this before, consider how Jesus regularly instructed His disciples to be different from the rest of the world. In John 17:14–16 (NASB), He said to His Father:

> I have given them Your word; and the world has hated them because they are not of the world, just as I am not of the world. I am not asking You to take them out of the world, but to keep them away from the evil one. They are not of the world, just as I am not of the world.

In a nutshell, if the world fits, then you're the wrong size.

James put it bluntly: "Do you not know that friendship with the world is hostility toward God?" (James 4:4 NASB).

As followers of Jesus, we can't settle for a faith that allows us to simply blend in and keep Christ in our back pockets in case of emergencies. Likewise, we can't teach our children this is how the Christian faith works, which begs these questions:

Are you parenting differently from the world around you?

Are your kids learning to think and live differently from the way the world thinks and lives?

Are you teaching your kids that following Jesus is a call to die to self—if necessary, literally (Matthew 16:24–25)?

Being set apart in this way won't happen automatically. The most natural human tendency is to assimilate into the world around us, and our kids feel this pressure every day. If we're not purposeful in our parenting, they'll follow along with whatever wave of culture is strongest at the time. And in this day and age, the culture's voice and influence are incredibly strong. Most parents (this writer included) can feel like we're losing this battle of leveraging our influence to be a louder voice than the world's.

If our kids are to become committed disciples of Jesus, we have to teach like Jesus did.

A REAL-LIFE PARENTING STORY

Teaching on Thursday Nights

For years, Kent and Lisa have made Thursday nights their evening to intentionally teach their kids a biblical principle or story. They make it a special—and easy—night by ordering pizza and using paper plates so they won't have much to clean up. Their goal is to make it a fun evening their kids will look forward to.

After finishing their pizza, they stay at the table and do an activity that connects with the principle or story they want to teach. (Plenty of resources online offer such activities.) Then they open their Bibles, read the applicable Scripture, and talk about it. When they're done, they play a favorite board game.

What's great about this model is that the principle they studied often comes up during the rest of the week, and they look for every opportunity to talk further about what they discussed on Thursday night. I applaud these parents and their strategy to systematically teach their kids the truths God wants them to know.

When a Parent Fails to Teach

Like a house that requires all its components to work effectively, our Discipling Home model requires attention to every element found in Jesus' example. As for the three pillars, if we model our faith and strive to apply, yet don't teach the ways of God as outlined in Scripture, something is missing.

Ultimately, our kids are left with *universalism*, the idea that all viewpoints and beliefs are valid. When it comes to issues of faith, universalism is summarized by the feel-good phrase *All roads lead to God*. On social issues and cultural trends, it's summarized by an attitude of *You be you, and I'll be me*. In this overwhelmingly common modern perspective, everything is gray and nothing is absolutely black or white, right or wrong. What's right for you might not be right for someone else, and that's totally okay.

This thinking has always been present in our culture, but it has absolutely overwhelmed us in recent years. Issues of sexuality and gender are the perfect example. Something the vast majority of our culture embraced as basic reality for centuries (a

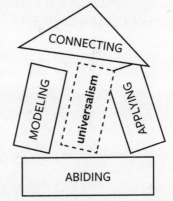

person with male sex organs is, by definition, a man, and a person with female genitalia and a womb is, by definition, a woman) is now open for debate. And that's just the tip of the iceberg regarding our culture's rejection of basic truth.

Gone are the days when parents can raise their kids in a Christian home and be confident that they're embracing their beliefs.

This is the world our kids are growing up in. Christian parents must choose to see universalism as an enemy that needs to be faced head-on with focus and tenacity.

Gone are the days when parents can raise their kids in a Christian home and be confident that they're embracing their beliefs. Recent studies have shown that many Christian teenagers ultimately walk away from their faith during high school or college—so many that it might be classified as a mass exodus. Multiple theories are offered for why this happens:

Are we connecting our kids merely to the church instead of to God?

Are we failing to introduce our kids to other faithful Christian adults who can reinforce what we're trying to teach them at home?

Are we foolishly counting on the osmosis method of discipleship?

The reality is that if we fail to teach what we believe and why we believe it, our kids will come to embrace what the world is offering.

Establishing an Environment for Spiritual Learning

We need a plan to start intentionally teaching our kids even if it's an imperfect one. If we aim at nothing, that's probably what we'll hit.

No matter your kids' ages, you can keep before you the goal of teaching them how to be mature disciples. Start by asking yourself, *What does the Bible have to say about values, morals, purity, purpose, money, goals, time management, friends, family, and the importance of a relationship with God?* Then teach them what it says in an age-appropriate way. Simply imagine what you want your kids to look like as mature adults and start doing what will get them there.

Teaching is both *deliberate* and *as you go*, and they can both be intentional.

As-You-Go Teaching

We like the idea of teaching as you go. Even the busiest parent can pray for, look for, and take advantage of teachable moments—for example, when your child learns something at school that allows you to share a biblical perspective. Or when your teenager is struggling with a difficult relationship, and you can help them consider what Jesus would have them do. Or when a way of thinking or living is displayed by a character in a movie or TV show you're watching or a book you're both reading. You have an opportunity to discuss the limitations of that perspective and if the Bible teaches a better way to live. These are teachable moments you can capitalize on.

Deliberate Teaching

While all the above are great places to share God's truth, He calls us as Christian parents to do far more than disciple on the fly. We can also be deliberate in teaching our children God's ways.

Dr. Rob Rienow of Visionary Family Ministries teaches often on this topic. I heard him speak to nearly six hundred parents over three different hours at my church, sharing the message that parents have a calling and responsibility to disciple the kids in their homes.

In the middle of his talk, he shared a little nugget of truth that was a game changer for many of the parents there, including me. It was the best advice on this critical aspect of parenting I've ever received. I'll tell you about it, but first, a little background.

Rob suggested that our homes can be "discipleship centers" where our main goal is to teach our children to know God and pursue Him as the primary focus of their lives. He pointed out the charge to parents found in Deuteronomy 6:7 (NASB): "Repeat [the truths of God] diligently to your sons and speak of them when you sit in your house, when you walk on the road, when you lie down, and when you get up."

In every hour he taught, he asked the group the same question: "When should we be teaching and discipling our kids?" In all three sessions, someone shouted out the answer "All the time!" Rob had to tell all three people they were wrong. He suggested that if we aren't currently doing anything to pour God's truth into our kids and then think God commands us to do it "all the time," we'll probably give up as failures before we even start. It's just too big of a task. His point wasn't that there are off-limit times for parents to connect with their kids but rather that God points parents to specific moments of great opportunity.

Then Rob took us back to Deuteronomy 6:7 and pointed out the four key, power-packed times God asks parents to teach spiritual truths to their kids. If we can focus on teaching during these four windows of time as opposed to the vague "all the time," we have a reasonable starting place to begin teaching like Jesus taught. Consider the possibilities of each one:

1. When You Sit in Your House—Intentional Times of Teaching

How hard would it be to have an intentional time when your family opens the Bible together and takes a few minutes to consider what it says? Not too hard. This can happen on a daily basis during family mealtimes when family members take turns bringing a Bible passage or principle to discuss. It can also happen once a week during a regularly scheduled family time.

The good people at Family Time Training (FamTime.com) offer tons of activity suggestions and resources to help you know what to talk about. Visionary Family Ministries also offers a free family worship resource at VisionaryFam.com /grace. Pro tip: the younger your kids are when you start practicing this discipline, the easier it will be to make it a normal part of your family rhythm.

2. When You Walk by the Way—or Ride in the Car

While few of us spend much time walking down the road with our kids, we spend plenty of time in the car—heading to school, church, appointments, or some activity. This can be the perfect time for brief discussions about the ways of Jesus. In fact, some conversations with your kids (especially your teenagers) can feel awkward when they're formal we-need-to-talk times. That's why the minutes you share with your kids as you cruise around town will be some of your best chances to teach.

3. When You Lie Down—Opportunity at Bedtime

Hopefully, you're already taking advantage of this third teaching prospect. With preschoolers, it might mean simply reading an age-appropriate Bible storybook as part of your bedtime routine. With older children, you might read a brief Bible passage and talk about what it means.

But with teenagers, teaching "when you lie down" will look a bit different. At our house, we found bedtime was when our adolescents most wanted to talk—usually at the foot of our bed when we wanted to go to sleep. Wise parents take advantage of these moments and step into whatever their kids want to talk about, looking for every chance to share a biblical worldview.

4. When You Rise Up—First Thing in the Morning

In addition to encouraging your kids to have their own brief quiet time with God at the start of each day, you can teach them in the morning in some simple ways:

- Share a quick verse from Proverbs and a brief application just before your kids head to school. This literally takes thirty seconds.
- Remind your children that God is with them. This can encourage them to face whatever challenges they encounter with courage.
- If you say grace before eating breakfast together, thank God for a recent family blessing as well as for the food.

Beginning each day with a brief moment of intentional teaching can have a huge impact.

Let me return to the great little nugget of parenting advice I hinted at earlier. As Rob Rienow taught the parents at my church, he shared a powerful quote by G. K. Chesterton that can encourage any struggling parent: "If a thing is worth doing, it is worth doing . . ."

When Rob paused after the word *doing*, the entire room responded with "Right." Because that's what we've always heard—"If it's worth doing, it's worth doing right."

But Rob's point was that we can dream about the "right" way to teach our kids, pray with them, and share spiritual truth with them, but usually our dream involves great big plans we never get to. Then we feel like inadequate failures before we even start, and we end up doing nothing.

Rob then revealed what G. K. Chesterton actually said: "If a thing is worth doing, it is worth doing badly."[3]

> *"If a thing is worth doing, it is worth doing badly."*
> —G. K. Chesterton

Here's the lesson I learned: if passing on spiritual truth to my kids is important (via reading the Word or reminding them of God's perspective or even just in praying for them and with them), then I want to start doing it immediately, even if I stink at it. It may be small. It may be simple. It may even be done badly. But I choose to start somewhere.

Is passing your faith on to your kids important to you? Then start doing it, even if it's through something as simple as a prayer on the way to school, a bedtime story from a Bible storybook, or a quick proverb texted to your teenager. As long as you do it with grace, care, and a bit of prayerful consideration, you'll be okay. And because this is one of those things God is passionate about, He will certainly be there with you.

The younger your children are when you start teaching them, the better, but you can start no matter how old they are. As your kids grow, you can encourage them to read and study on their own, making yourself readily available to help them process what they're learning.

Two last things:

First, don't freak out if your children start to question what you're teaching them. As they hit adolescence and begin to move from concrete to abstract reasoning—and the questions that accompany that—doubt can be both natural and good. Remember that Jesus was once an adolescent, and the one Bible story we have of Him during that season contains His very first spoken word. It was a question He asked His parents: "Why?" (Look it up in Luke 2:49.) When your kids start asking why, take a deep breath and relax. It's a chance for them to process the truth at a deeper level, hopefully with your guidance.

And second, it's wise to regularly evaluate where and how and why you're spending your parenting energies. We spend a ton of energy on things that by comparison don't matter all that much in God's agenda for our kids. (You can evaluate your own life and schedule here, but sports and other extracurricular activities that are exhausting you might come to your mind.)

At the end of the day, know that the burden of responsibility to teach your kids what it means to follow Jesus is on you. And while you may feel ill-equipped for the task, the reality is that any parent can do it. Your effort doesn't have to be grandiose. It can be simple. Just make it authentic and in the context of relationship. Give yourself room to crawl before you walk.

"If discipleship in your home is worth doing, it's worth doing badly." That's great advice for every parent.

FOR PERSONAL
Reflection

- Read Proverbs 22:6.
- Why is it so important to intentionally train your kids as you disciple them at home?
- Jot down one way you can take advantage of each of these four power-packed times to teach your kids:

  1. When you sit in your house—intentional times of teaching
  2. When you walk by the way—or ride in the car

3. When you lie down—opportunity at bedtime
4. When you rise up—first thing in the morning

- Pray now, asking God to show you teachable moments you can step into every day. Then ask Him for boldness to take those steps.

APPLYING

Giving Your Children Opportunities to Live Out Their Faith

The faith of the average eighteen-year-old is kind of like his seventh grade science project. Mom and Dad did all the work and he just put his name on it.

—Neil McClendon[1]

We all know the kid. He's active at church, has faithful attendance in Sunday school, and probably knows a lot of Bible verses by memory. But he's still a jerk. He's self-centered, mean, and the type of kid you don't want yours to be around. He would claim to be a Christian even though there's absolutely zero evidence in his life that God is making a difference in who he is.

If we're honest, we have to admit we know plenty of "Christian" adults like this as well. Whether you know them in person or interact with them on social media, church people can be the meanest people on the planet. It's as if what they know about God and who Christ has called them to be never settles into their hearts. They may claim to be followers of Jesus, but they don't look or act anything like Him.

The accepted standards of Christian life in the twenty-first-century western church can often look radically different from what Jesus called the disciples to live out. Many Christians—particularly in the Bible Belt—have become tolerant of a form of cultural Christianity, where attending church services and giving lip service to a biblical worldview is the norm. Church participation is seen as just one part of the American Dream and as a help to anyone who wants to be a good person.

Again, this is a far cry from the call of radical discipleship Jesus invited His followers into. We're asked to accept His gift of grace, allow Him to transform us into His image, and then join Him in His mission to redeem the world. But this isn't the message most of our kids are getting. They see the Christian life as something else entirely.

It's what Christian Smith of the University of North Carolina Chapel Hill discovered in his study of the faith of American teenagers back in 2005 and published in his book *Soul Searching*. Through all his research, he learned that most of the kids plugged into our churches generally see the Christian faith as what he called "moralistic therapeutic deism."

Smith found that most teens believe Christianity is about embracing a moralistic approach to life: "It teaches that central to living a good and happy life is being a good, moral person. That means being nice, kind, pleasant, respectful, responsible, at work on self-improvement, taking care of one's health, and doing one's best to be successful."[2]

Once more, this is profoundly different from what the Bible teaches. The core of true discipleship—taking up one's cross to follow Jesus wherever He leads—is a foreign concept to most of our churched youth.

As I've interacted with thousands of teenagers in the local church through the years, I've learned that most are living the Christian life only in theory. Sure, they know what they're supposed to do because they've heard it over and over again at church, but they don't actually do it. It's as if the majority of our church kids hear the truth and then agree to wink at one another on the way out of the building as if to say, "Yeah, but not really."

Something is missing in our attempt to pass on the faith to the next generation. With so many young people leaving the church once they graduate from high school, we've got to consider why the truths we're striving to teach them aren't sticking. Going back to our discipleship model, maybe we're modeling and teaching, but we aren't actually giving our kids a chance to truly live out their faith.

Faith without Works Is Dead

The call to follow Jesus is a call to life change and action. Sure, the Christian life is at its core a relationship with God. As I said before, we're human beings not human doings. But if walking with Jesus doesn't change our priorities and our purpose in life, then we're missing the point.

James wrote at length about how our faith will drive our actions:

> Do not merely listen to the word, and so deceive yourselves. Do what it says. Anyone who listens to the word but does not do what it says is like someone who looks at his face in a mirror and, after looking at himself, goes away and immediately forgets what he looks like. But whoever looks intently into the perfect law that gives freedom, and continues in it—not forgetting what they have heard, but doing it—they will be blessed in what they do.
>
> James 1:22–25

Millions of kids—and I dare say millions of adults—reflect on the truths of Jesus at church every Sunday and then walk out the door without any real plan to change or act on what they heard. There's no action or experience of living out a Spirit-filled life.

The bottom line for parents is this: if your child is that jerk-faced church kid, something is off. If your teenager claims to be a Christian but there's no evidence that Jesus is affecting their life or worldview, something is wrong. The point of teaching is life change. If you're not seeing that, then something might be missing in how you're teaching.

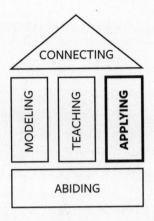

How do we disciple our kids so real transformation takes place? The answer to that question is found by looking at how Jesus did it with the Twelve. Our Discipling Home model shows us the critical need for *application*—putting faith into actual practice.

While Jesus actively modeled and taught, a key part of His discipleship strategy involved intentionally sending His disciples out into the world on mission. We see this in many places in the Gospels and certainly in the book of Acts.

Here's an example from the book of Luke:

> When Jesus had called the Twelve together, he gave them power and authority to drive out all demons and to cure diseases, and he sent them out to proclaim the kingdom of God and to heal the sick. He told them: "Take nothing for the journey—no staff, no bag, no bread, no money, no extra shirt. Whatever house you enter, stay there until you leave that town. If people do not welcome you, leave their town and shake the dust off your feet as a testimony against them." So

they set out and went from village to village, proclaiming the good news and healing people everywhere.

Luke 9:1–6

Sending the disciples out instantly moved Jesus' teaching from theory to activity. It provided the context for them to learn, experience, and be coached. This is what discipleship is: putting into practice what you claim to believe. It's far more than head knowledge; it's life change. Simply put, young disciples need opportunities to live out their faith, and parents must intentionally provide these opportunities.

This story continues, "When the apostles returned, they reported to Jesus what they had done. Then he took them with him and they withdrew by themselves to a town called Bethsaida" (Luke 9:10).

Once Jesus' disciples had their experiences and returned to Him with what were likely stories of both successes and failures along the way, we can be sure that He coached and encouraged them. The feedback and accountability likely helped them learn to put their faith into practice and integrate the ways of Jesus into their everyday lives.

If you read the account of this time Jesus had with the Twelve in Matthew 10, you'll see even more about His instructions. He told the disciples they would be doing amazing work. He also warned them it would be hard—they would be persecuted. There was good news, as well, though: the Spirit of God would speak through them and give them exactly what they needed in the moment.

The disciples had a chance to truly experience God at work in and through them personally. Our kids need this as well—moving faith in God from theory to reality. As we've already said, too many of our kids spend eighteen years connecting with church but never truly experiencing God. This application component is our chance to give our kids that opportunity.

Experience Is Far Better Than Book Learning

Back in the mid-twentieth century, Edgar Dale created the "Cone of Experience" learning model, which claims people remember little of what they read, a bit more of what they see and hear, and in many cases a whole lot of what they experience.[3] While some educators and researchers have questioned this model,[4] we can't deny the value of on-the-job training, particularly if our goal is transformation and not merely education. (Note to parents: that's your goal. You don't want your kids to just know stuff; you want them to experience a changed life found in Christ.)

When my kids were young, I took an international mission trip to Zimbabwe. With my own eyes, I saw the needs of the people and amazing ways God was working there. It was absolutely life changing. When I got home and shared my experiences with my kids and showed them photos and videos, they were polite enough to listen and be excited for me, but I don't think they felt what I did.

Fast-forward a few years to when my kids became teenagers and we were able to introduce them to the world beyond the safe and insulated bubble in which we were raising them. We invited them to join us in various opportunities to serve the marginalized and less fortunate people in our city and world. Once they began to see the incredible needs of their fellow humans with their own eyes and then joined God in meeting those needs, they got it. It changed everything for them.

In the doing is where faith in God becomes real to our kids. All that head knowledge is meaningless if they don't have the chance to apply it.

Putting what your kids know into practice can always be in the center of your mind. And the level of commitment, expectation, and risk can grow in significance as they get older. We can continually be looking for opportunities for them to live out their faith in the world. As a parent wanting to help your kids own their faith, your role will shift from coach to trainer as they age, helping them learn and process what they're experiencing. Too many parents don't make that transition, operating as helicopter parents, controlling every choice their teenagers make, never allowing them to fail.

As your kids grow and mature, the teaching block—while always there—grows smaller. You're trying to work yourself out of a job, making your children more dependent on Jesus and less on you. Quicker than you can ever imagine, the day will come when you won't be there to guide them at all. John the Baptist's declaration about Jesus in John 3:30—"He must become greater; I must become less"— applies here as well. Your goal is to make yourself less and less necessary in your child's spiritual life.

> *You're trying to work yourself out of a job, making your children more dependent on Jesus and less on you.*

You can't expect your kids to know what you know at a meaningful level, especially since they don't have the experience you have. That's why you need to give experience to them. If we don't, we'll one day launch young adults into the world who know a lot about Jesus but have never truly seen Him at work in their lives.

When Kids Don't Learn to Apply What They're Learning

If our kids learn a lot about God but it doesn't fundamentally change who they are or how they act, then we're not making disciples of Jesus. We're creating Bible scholars with no real faith, spiritually dead inside. Sure, they can score big at Bible trivia, but they look nothing like the One they're claiming to follow. Sound familiar? The Pharisees in Jesus' time were like this, and He had some pretty harsh words for them.

This type of Christianity can best be characterized as dead religion. It's found in those with a biblical belief system but no real change of heart. The fruit of God's work in our lives is "love, joy, peace, patience, kindness, goodness, faithfulness, gentleness, self-control" (Galatians 5:22–23 ESV). We

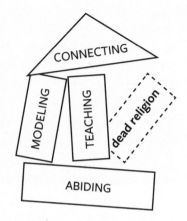

all know people who claim to follow Christ but seem void of these fundamental characteristics.

Paul gives Timothy a stern warning about people like these, saying they're "always learning but never able to come to a knowledge of the truth" (2 Timothy 3:7). Read verses 1–6 to learn more about people like this. It's not pretty.

Some people who know the Bible best have somehow failed to let it penetrate into their hearts and change their character. Maybe they take pride in having knowledge, or maybe they simply like using legalism to control others. You've probably run into these folks on social media, trolling others' posts, always looking to pick a theological fight. Sure, they're passionate about their perspective, but you see very little indication of Jesus' love in them. They think they're doing the Lord's work, but my gut says they're moving others further from God, not closer.

When it comes to our kids' generation, too many Christian young people are raised to know the Word but not be transformed by it. They see the Bible as a collection of rules and are rarely given a chance to see God's goodness. So when they encounter a world that runs contrary to God's truth—and they run into those blowhard trolls on social media—the Scriptures aren't seen as life-giving. They're seen as repressive.

At its core, we can teach our kids that God's law as shown in the Bible is simply a road map of how He made the world to work. If we follow it, there will be peace in our lives. If we don't follow it, there will be turmoil. Through experience, our children must see the fruit of God's ways. If we don't give them that chance, an entire generation won't believe His ways are best. And their faith won't last.

In summary, many of the children and youth we're bringing up in the church are learning a lot about Jesus, but they never truly have the chance to "taste and see that the LORD is good" (Psalm 34:8). This can come only through action, taking risky steps of faith, and seeing God show up in both big and small ways.

Again, this will likely not happen just because your family is active in your church. Even if your kids are there every time the doors open—though that's almost unheard of with our busy schedules today—they're likely learning truth but rarely given chances to put it into practice. Each week has 168 hours. Given that the church may have your

A REAL-LIFE PARENTING STORY

Involving Kids in Ministry

In chapter 1, I mentioned that I was recently diagnosed with cancer. As you might expect, we've been flooded with cards from friends letting us know they're praying for us. One card stands out to me.

A young couple we know from the big marriage conference we host every fall not only started praying but told my story to their young kids so they could all be praying as a family. Their five-year-old son wanted to send me a note to let me know about his prayers, so he colored a card and his mom wrote out his words. He also included a small balloon in the envelope as a gift.

kids for just one hour and you have them for the other 167 (and yes, I'm counting the time they spend anywhere but at church—even school), the burden of this falls squarely on you.

So how can a parent step into this world of application in the discipleship process?

I wanted to affirm the steps he took, so I sent an email to him via his mom's address, telling him how much I appreciated what he sent. I included a photo of me holding the inflated balloon and said how happy it made me to carry it to my radiation appointment that day. (A silly move for an adult, but a logical one for a kindergartener.)

The mom responded that the note absolutely made her son's week. That was exactly my intention: I wanted to affirm that praying for and caring for others in the name of Jesus was the most important thing this little boy could possibly do.

I hope he had the chance to experience God at work through him in a way that makes him want to do it again. These small steps of obedience help build a lasting faith.

Create a Lab Where Kids Can Experiment with Their Faith

The ways you can give your children opportunities to put their faith into practice are limitless. And if you're open to Him, the creative God who loves you and leads you will show you what to do.

Consider the following ways you can start helping your kids apply what they know:

Be ready to stop everything and pray. When a need presents itself, get your children into the habit of praying about it right then. If God is with us everywhere we go, then why wouldn't we take our needs to Him the minute they pop up? Let seeking God and His perspective on the daily issues of your lives be the norm in your home.

See your neighborhood as your mission field. Your kids may not be able to take Jesus to the nations yet, but through you, they can begin to see their community as a place where God is at work. When it comes to the people you interact with on a regular basis, ask yourself simple questions like, *How can I show them the love of Jesus?* If you have people in your lives who don't know Jesus (and there should be), then what you do and how you live communicates to them—and to your children—who God is.

When you serve others, let your kids join you. As you care for others' needs in the church and community, invite your children to take part. We remember fondly those times we took a meal to or cleaned the home of a family dealing with illness. When we pulled away from their house, our kids were exhausted from all the work they did, but they were also asking what else we could do to help. They found joy in serving and loving like Jesus.

Help your kids experience selflessness and sacrifice. Like my example above, whenever you can, give your kids opportunities to do things where they get nothing in return. While it's completely normal for us to ask, *What's in it for me?* your kids need to learn that a fundamental component of following Jesus is that it's not about what you get; it's about what you give. Christ modeled this well, making the ultimate sacrifice of His very life.

Look for application opportunities as you interact with media. As you watch TV, the news, or view content on social media, ask God for teachable moments. When you see lifestyles, decisions, or attitudes that run contrary to God's best, talk about the fruit of a life in rebellion against God versus one that submits to Him. Use discernment with this, but don't totally insulate your kids from the world's perspective. See exposure to it as a chance to discuss and apply God's truths.

Take a family mission trip. A family trip focused on the needs of others is a great way to get your kids out of their comfort zone and seeing God at work. When they can join Him and take part in an intentional mission-minded endeavor, something amazing happens. While you pray for fruit from your own work, some of the best fruit will come in the lives of your kids.

Always study the Bible with application in mind. If we think the purpose of Bible study is to learn more about the Bible, then we're missing the point. Again, life change is the goal. Teach your kids to study the Bible, and then after reading a passage, write down responses to three simple questions in a notebook or journal:

What?
So what?
Now what?

And here's how they can respond to each question:

What? Jot down a quick summary of what the passage is saying—just the facts.

So what? Write a few things they feel God might be telling them—and make it personal.

Now what? Respond to God's truth with something actionable. Based on what the passage says and what it means to them, the "Now what?" response is how they'll learn to put their faith into action, and their lives will start to transform.

Every part of our five-part Discipling Home model is essential. But this application component is the most critical because it's probably the most neglected. If we fail to give our kids the chance to live out their faith, they'll never actually experience a transformed life in Christ.

This sanctification (or growth) process will take place all throughout your kids' lives, but they can get into the habit of experiencing it now. For those eighteen years or so they're under your roof, you can help them see that Jesus can be actively at work in their lives every day through actually living out God's ways.

That can be the goal of every parent when it comes to discipling their children. We want to see our kids thinking like Jesus, talking like Jesus, loving like Jesus, and becoming more and more like Him every day. The application of what we're teaching them is where this actually happens.

FOR PERSONAL
Reflection

- Read James 1:22.
- Why is it so important to give your kids opportunities to become "doers of the Word" as you disciple them?
- What are two or three ways you can practice this principle in your daily life at home? For example, identifying a neighbor who needs the care or ministry your family can provide.
- Ask God to help you creatively connect the truths you're teaching your children to actual opportunities where they can apply what they're learning.

seven
CONNECTING

Developing and Maintaining a Love Relationship with Your Children

---

As the Father has loved me, so have I loved you. Now remain in my love.

—Jesus, John 15:9

A few years back, Jenifer and I sat in a conference with respected Bible teachers Stuart and Jill Briscoe. This amazing couple, who at the time were close to eighty years old, had much to say about the lessons they learned throughout their years of parenting. I clearly remember Jill casually stressing the importance of the connection between a parent and child:

"You want them to like you. If they don't like you, they won't listen to you. After all, do you listen to people you don't like?"[1]

Our eyes were immediately opened to a fundamental truth about raising the kids God had entrusted to us: the love relationship we share with them is perhaps our most valuable commodity. Sure, we love them and they love us, but is there warmth there? Do we genuinely like each other? Do we enjoy spending time together?

The love relationship between you and your children is the gasoline that keeps the parental influence engine in your home fueled. It's a dynamic that can and must be established, nurtured, and then meticulously maintained throughout the ups and downs of a child's development. While it would be nice if they pitched in, we absolutely cannot count on our kids to do any of this work. We parents have the sole responsibility of fostering an environment that communicates how much we love and value them every day.

As your kids get older, they'll naturally begin to pull away. Peer relationships tend to replace the parent-and-child relationship as the one that gets most of their emotional attention and energy. That's totally normal and okay. Still, their relationship with their parents needs to be strong and rich to successfully navigate adolescence. Parents who connect with and then nurture their teens' hearts will discover that their influence still overrides the influence of their teens' peers.

Much has been said about parents being parents, not their children's friends. Experts agree that one of the biggest mistakes parents can make is striving too hard to be their child's buddy. While I agree with this sentiment, the result for some has been an extreme swing in the wrong direction—parents making it their goal to remain emotionally disconnected from their kids. As one father I heard put it, "My goal with my teenagers is to make sure they don't like me." I think he's totally missing the point.

The Love Relationship Is Critical

The final part of our Discipling Home model is *connecting*. This concept accentuates the vital importance of the love relationship between you and your child. It's illustrated here as the roof of our allegorical house. This is a perfect fit. Just as a roof secures and protects your home from the elements, the relationships you create and maintain within your home cover an endless multitude of failures and shortcomings. You may not be a perfect parent, but if there's love in your home, chances are good that you'll get through it all.

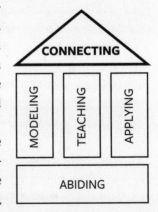

We can see the importance of connecting in the discipleship ministry Jesus had with the Twelve. Sure, He modeled, taught, and sent His disciples, but He did it all in the context of relationship. He spent three years close to them, spending endless amounts of time with them, sharing everything. And His teaching impact was maximized through this love relationship.

In fact, it's the relational aspect of the process that most defines Jesus' teaching style. He articulated this in John 15:14–15: "You are my friends if you do what I command. I no longer call you servants, because a servant does not know his master's business. Instead, I have called you friends, for everything that I learned from my Father I have made known to you."

Note that Jesus called them friends, with an implied level of closeness and affection, because He shared so many intimate details of kingdom living with them.

Why is the heart relationship between parent and child—as with leader and disciple—so important?

- Because that affectionate love relationship you share with your kids will leverage your teaching and increase its impact by a huge multiplier.
- Because it will increase your joy in striving to teach for life change, which can be an exhausting process.
- Because it's somehow a fundamental part of God's work of grace in and through humanity.

This last point is illustrated perfectly within Scripture, ending the Old Testament and opening the New Testament. The very last verse in the Old Testament is Malachi 4:6. It gives a prophecy about the ministry of a new Elijah who will "turn the hearts of the parents to their children, and the hearts of the children to their parents." When all has been said and done in the old covenant, this is the final word God gives us.

Then after four hundred years of silence, at the very beginning of the New Testament we see another reference to this new Elijah, whom we learn is John the Baptist. There in Luke 1:17, it similarly says that he will "turn the hearts of the parents to their children and the disobedient to the wisdom of the righteous—to make ready a people prepared for the Lord."

The Old Testament ends with this theme, and the Gospels open with it. What is evident is that one element critical to the ushering in of the kingdom of God is the heart connection between parent and child. This love relationship is the primary means by which our faith is passed from one generation to the next. When the love relationship is severed or broken, our ability to influence the next generation is limited. But when it's nurtured to be strong, our influence is great.

> *One element critical to the ushering in of the kingdom of God is the heart connection between parent and child.*

Granted, this is easy when our kids are young, and it gets harder as they grow older. When my children were little, having their hearts was easy. They thought their mom and dad were fun and cool. Being together was a joy for both us and the kids. From their perspective, they knew they were utterly dependent on us. In practical terms, we were their ticket to the good life. Staying close to us relationally guaranteed them fun, activities, bedtime stories, Happy Meals from the drive-through, and the occasional trip to Disney World. Crawling up on our laps for cuddles was a regular occurrence.

When they moved into adolescence, we saw a change. What could once be done on autopilot—building and maintaining a love relationship—now required work on our part. And it was heavy lifting, requiring discernment and tenacity as well as plenty of *God, help me* prayers. As parents, it was much harder to connect with teens whose actions, words, and attitudes communicated that they no longer had much use for us.

But just because it was hard doesn't mean it wasn't critically important. Even though it becomes more challenging to stay connected to your kids as they get older, do whatever it takes to accomplish it. Push past their resistant exteriors and reach their hearts, all because the rewards are worth it. Jesus did it with the Twelve, so we're invited to prioritize this connection with our children.

When the Relationship Is Weak, Rebellion Can Flourish

We all know families led by well-intentioned parents who seem to do everything right, but then their children walk away from the faith sometime during adolescence. What gives? While no formulas with guaranteed results exist, my experience suggests that one thing missing is a powerful love relationship between parents and kids.

Even though we think we're communicating unconditional love to them, most of our children—particularly teenagers—don't feel it. They want to believe their parents will love them "no matter what," but studies suggest that many of them doubt that's true. Within their insecure minds, they play out hypothetical scenarios and become convinced of this: *if I were to do* that, *surely my parents wouldn't love me.*

This is why so many kids flock to their peer relationships the minute they're given that freedom. They reason that while their parents aren't fully safe, their friends are. *They accept me for who I am.* Obviously, this isn't fair. Teenage peers don't have to discipline or correct or make them clean their rooms or do their homework.

When the love relationship between parent and child isn't firing on all cylinders, there's no real motivation for a kid to embrace the truths embraced by the parent. Our desire to teach a Christian worldview or the vital importance of a relationship with God falls apart. Our kids reject what we most want to communicate to them. In keeping with our house motif, it's like building a solid house with huge holes in the roof. Everything is compromised. And it's likely to lead to some form of rebellion.

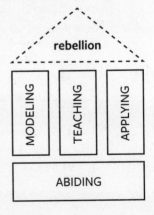

A REAL-LIFE PARENTING STORY

"Teenagers Are My Jam"

Our friends Kathy and Jerry have five children spread fourteen years apart. While they would admit they're imperfect parents, they've worked hard to stay connected to their kids as each one moved from being a child to a teenager, finding ways to savor and enjoy the crazy adolescent years.

In fact, Kathy often says, "Teenagers are my jam." Where most parents struggle, she and Jerry are thriving. From carving out one-on-one time with their kids, to making their house the go-to "hang out" for their teens' peers, they make connecting with their teenagers a priority.

Yes, it's messy, but it's paying huge dividends. They've launched four of their children into college and adulthood, and I'm amazed at how much those kids still seem to gravitate toward home and their parents. They want to be there all because Kathy and Jerry intentionally focused on and evolved the relationship as their kids grew up. Their continued influence on them is strong all because they chose to actively pursue their teenagers' hearts.

There's a delicate dimension of parenting that, if not kept intact, will totally undermine your influence with your kids. Again, this is usually easy to foster with younger children but becomes harder with teenagers. It's a basic subconscious belief in the mind of your child that says *my parents want what's best for me—they do the crazy things they do because they love me.*

I'm operating on the assumption that you do in fact want what's best for your kids. (You're not really crazy.) Acting on this noble desire for your kids will regularly require you to do things that are uncomfortable for them. When you have to discipline them, they won't like it. They might argue. They might roll their eyes. They'll even resist correction at times.

Despite this, though, you hope that somewhere in the inner reaches of their brains they're clinging to the fact that Mom and Dad are doing this for their good. They subconsciously believe that, as the author of Hebrews said, "No discipline seems pleasant at the time, but painful. Later on, however, it produces a harvest of righteousness and peace for those who have been trained by it" (Hebrews 12:11). In other words, you're sometimes required to be hard on your kids now so life will go well for them in the future.

In contrast, as some kids move through the challenges of adolescence, they begin to truly doubt that their parents are acting in their best interests. They come to believe that their parents are mean, wanting them to suffer, and not at all motivated by love. Once their brains land there, all bets are off for parental leadership and influence. Those kids have the real potential to implode their lives and take everyone else down with them in the process.

So what is the superpower that enables parents to keep their kids believing that Mom and Dad are acting in their best interest? Love. Creating, developing, and maintaining the love relationship is what will convince disciplined or punished kids that their parents still want the best for them. And in most every case, it will keep them from significantly derailing their lives.

Build Bridges to Your Child's Heart

As you might know from your own experience, building bridges to your child's heart is easy when they're young and a bit harder when they're teenagers. Simply put, your goal with littles is to build the love relationship, and your goal with adolescents is to work tenaciously to maintain it.

If you want to build good patterns with your young children, here are a few places to start:

Get on your child's level. It's hard for a little person to connect with a big person if the big person is always "over them." Certainly, you'll want to parent from a place of authority, but when talking about their feelings, schoolwork, or something creative they've done, kneel or sit down where you can see eye to eye.

Take an interest in what's interesting to them. If some activity piques your kid's interest and gives them joy, spend time doing that thing together. Nothing connects people better than a shared passion. Even if you don't understand their stuff, be curious and ask questions. And if you think whatever they're interested in is, well, stupid, then fake interest. This is the uncomfortable, heavy lifting of parenthood, but you can do it.

Laugh—a lot. Look for the random, funny things in everyday life that get you both tickled, and then step into the ridiculousness. Laughter releases wonderful endorphins that connect two people quicker than just about anything. One caveat: get used to laughing at some really dumb stuff, because let's face it, the average preschooler's sense of humor isn't very refined. Boogers and poop are sometimes hilarious to them.

Figure out their "love language." Gary Chapman's seminal book *The 5 Love Languages* has been helpful for millions of marriages, but it provides excellent insights for parents as well. Try to figure out if your child responds best to quality time, words of affirmation, receiving gifts, acts of service, or physical touch.[2] Once you think you have their love language dialed in, look for every opportunity to speak it. (Chapman has also written *The 5 Love Languages of Children* with coauthor Ross Campbell and *The 5 Love Languages of Teenagers*.)

Share memorable experiences. Making memories together helps you dig down deep into the relationship well so you can draw from those memories as your kids get older. Find activities, vacations, and routines everyone enjoys and do them as often as you can. Your kids will collect good memories where you're a critical participant and value you as part of their lives.

Step carefully into their hurts, fears, and other painful emotions. Be there for your kids when they're processing through key emotional moments that will likely be burned into their brains for a long time. Remembering your being close by and empathetic during challenging times will stick with them and connect you deeply. In contrast, if they remember bad emotions and have memories where your response made things worse, resentment and disconnection will grow. And you don't want that.

Get off your phone and be present. One key to effective parenting in today's world is simply putting down your phone. We talk a lot about our kids' bad smartphone habits, but parents set the pace. Ask the people you love if you're on your phone too much, and then listen to their answers without getting defensive. Maybe it's time to make a change. You'll be well on your way to being an incredible parent if you'll simply be present.

If You Have Teenagers, Work Hard to Nurture the Relationship

Again, as your kids make the transition into adolescence, which starts earlier than ever before, they'll likely begin to pull away from you a bit. Or a lot. Don't interpret this as rejection. They're simply finding their way in the larger world of their peers. This is a good and healthy transition that will serve them well through life.

If you take their move away from you personally, you're likely to build resentment and make them feel guilty for treating you "poorly." Yes, you can have and require some fundamental expectations of respect, but their hormonal attitudes will be challenging for a while. Maybe for five or six years.

Lucky you.

To get through that harrowing season, your kids want to be regularly bathed in the unconditional love you have for them. This will require God-sized patience and longsuffering on your part. As far back as 2008, a *Psychology Today* article said, "The average high school kid today has the same level of anxiety as the average psychiatric patient in the early 1950s" and "We are getting more anxious every decade."[3]

Ouch.

Here are some best practices to help you connect with your teen's heart:

Celebrate what's unique about them. Too many parents freak out when their teen develops a radically different personality than theirs. It's as if the parent assumes the way *they* think and act and behave is normal and anything else is unacceptable. Give your teen time to find out who they are even if who they're becoming is different from you. Also know they may try on dozens of different personas throughout adolescence. Just because they go Goth for a season doesn't mean they'll stay there forever. Take it easy and love them well. (Also revisit the love languages mentioned earlier.)

Get into their world. Just as it's wise when your child is younger, take an interest in what interests your teen. It's a great way to draw closer. One of my sons has an acute interest in the world of superheroes and comic books. I've taken the occasional deep dive into that space, not because I care as much about the content, but because I care about my son. The payoff for our relationship is totally worth it. Find those things that excite your teenager and be curious.

Recognize the power of shoulder-to-shoulder time. If you want your teen to talk to you, it probably won't happen if you say to them, "Let's sit down, look at each other, and talk." That feels more like a lecture to them than a two-way conversation. Teens are more likely to open up in a shoulder-to-shoulder position when they don't have to be eye to eye with you. This is why drives in the car can be powerful connection times. See every moment you're alone in the car with them as a chance to build the relationship—even if it's in a small way.

Close your mouth. Too many parents want to dominate conversations because they believe they're wise and their kids are foolish. They figure their words have more weight. This thinking will help you win an argument, but it will do nothing to connect you to the heart of your teen. Constantly consider what's most valuable to you—being right or being close. If you truly want to have your teen's heart (where your long-term impact will be multiplied), ask a lot of questions. Then listen with interest, empathy, and compassion.

Offer plenty of grace. Being a teenager is hard, and your kids need your grace to figure it out. It helps to remember that you've been given immeasurable grace from an incredibly patient God. Keeping this truth in mind will enable you to be a better agent of grace in your teen's life.

My wife, Jenifer, offered "do-overs" to our teens. When they said something disrespectful or handled a situation poorly, instead of immediately correcting or punishing them, she'd simply say, "Do you want a do-over?" It was a gracious offer for them to reload and try handling whatever it was differently to avoid a consequence. It diffused the situation and provided some of the best-learned lessons for our kids.

Be willing to say you're sorry. Nothing undermines our credibility with our teenagers like not admitting when we're wrong. When they know we're at fault but too prideful to humble ourselves and apologize, it drives a huge wall between us and them. In contrast, nothing will build bridges like honest vulnerability and humility that declares *I am in need of God's grace just like you are.*

Delight in them. When your kids enter a room or you see them after school, what's the typical vibe they get from you? It likely falls into one of three categories: frustration, indifference, or delight. At any given moment, your teens have the impression that you're either not pleased with them (frustrated), couldn't care less about them (indifferent), or happy to be with them (delighted).

Obviously, your goal is to communicate delight. You want them to know that even though your relationship can experience challenging moments, they still bring you immeasurable joy. Communicate delight by your words, tone, and actions, and a teen will gravitate toward that.

How to Know If You're Connected to Your Kids

Do you have your teenager's heart? A simple little litmus test will tell you a great deal.

Imagine your teen is out with friends on a Friday night and is tempted to participate in some immoral activity—or at least an ill-advised and illegal one like underage drinking. At this moment of decision, one of two possible thoughts will go through their mind:

1. If my parents find out about this, they'll kill me.
2. If my parents find out about this, it will kill them.[4]

Notice the subtle difference? The first thought shows the kid is most worried about a possible punishment. The second thought shows the kid is most concerned about breaking their parents' hearts, most likely because the relationship has been nurtured and developed into something the teenager values and doesn't want to damage. (Note to parents: the goal is for your kids to have the latter thought.)

Pursuing the hearts of our kids is a journey that never stops. Furthermore, just as getting in shape is a lot harder than staying in shape, keeping a child's heart is much easier than trying to recapture it once it's gone. Wise parents who want to influence their kids will focus on building and nurturing a powerful love connection with them—one that evolves and changes as their children get older, yet stays intact.

Finally, don't forget the foundation of our discipleship model (abiding), as it's essential to the roof (connecting). If you want to build a love relationship with your child but you don't know how, try asking God what's really going on in their hearts and minds. He is ever close to you. He's willing and able to give you insights into how to meet your child's every need.

Just ask Him. Listen for His voice. He truly wants to lead you to be an incredible and impactful parent as you lead and disciple your kids.

FOR PERSONAL
Reflection

- Read 1 Thessalonians 2:8.
- How vital do you think the love relationship is to passing on eternal truths (the gospel) to your kids? How are you making that assessment?

149

- Do you know families who seem very close? What do they do to make that possible? What can you learn from them?

- How would you evaluate the heart connection you have with each of your kids? What makes your relationship better? What makes it worse?

- What are two or three practical steps you can take in the short term to better connect with each of your children? For example, perhaps you can start by identifying their love languages and do something simple to act on them. And be sure to ask God for ideas specific to His agenda for your family.

- Ask God to give you discernment and insight into how loved by you each of your kids feel. Then ask Him to give you tangible and specific ways you can reach their hearts.

eight

NOW GO MAKE DISCIPLES

Making disciples is far more than a program. It is the mission of our lives. It defines us. A disciple is a disciple maker.

—*Francis Chan*[1]

Congratulations on making it to the end of this book! All this has probably been a lot to take in, and you may feel overwhelmed by, or even scared by, the challenge before you as a parent. "Doing what Jesus did" might seem like an insurmountable task. But I encourage you to take a deep breath and begin to believe you can do what God calls you to do. You may not be perfect, but you can be successful. You may not have what it takes, but God does. And He's on your side.

I love what Paul writes in Ephesians 5:1: "Be imitators of God, as beloved children" (ESV). The first part of that verse is scary, but the second part is empowering. We think, *There's no way I can do what Jesus did.* But the second part holds the key: "as beloved children." There's a truth there you can embrace.

The most natural thing in the world is for your kids to grow up to physically look like you because they carry your genes.

Because you're God's child, slowly growing into His image, He's fully invested in you. He's always with you. And He's always for you.

May I remind you that when you were born again in Christ, God's genes were deposited into you? Jesus' identity as a sinless, Spirit-filled agent of God became your new identity. It's who you now are. And the most natural thing in the world is for you to grow to become more and more like your Father every day.

If God is calling you to be a discipler of your kids (and He is), then He will lead you and empower you to pull it off. If only you'll ask Him, He'll guide and help you every step along the way. Because you're God's child, slowly growing into His image, He's fully invested in you. He's always with you. And He's always for you.

Let God Do the Work Through You

Do you remember my golf illustration back in chapter 2? About how I'm sure I would be a pretty good golfer if I could emulate everything Tiger Woods does on the golf course? I invite you to consider taking that illustration one step further.

Let's say I was invited to play in a competitive golf tournament with a cash prize, and I wanted to play the best golf of my life. Instead of thinking *I want to copy Tiger Woods*, what if there were a way he could literally play through me?

Wouldn't it be awesome if I could somehow unzip my skin and Tiger Woods would crawl into my body and wear me sort of like a body suit? (You may have seen Wile E. Coyote do this with a sheep's costume back when you were a kid.) Then I could zip myself back up so people couldn't see that Tiger was actually the one playing the game. In that scenario, I wouldn't be just copying Tiger; he'd be literally doing the work, and I'd just be going along for the ride. In that tournament, how could I lose?

This is not unlike the Spirit-filled life God has called us to. Each of the five elements of our discipleship model are essential, but it starts with the foundation—your staying close to God. So close that it's not unlike His moving and leading and working through you.

God wants to see your kids walking with Him, and He wants to use you to lead them. All He requires is that you lay down your personal agenda for your kids and yield to His. Then join Him in the discipleship process. Remember that He has a voice, and He wants to show you what to do. More importantly, He wants to do the work in and through you.

Four Common Questions from Parents

As I've shared the principles of The Discipling Home in live teachings with parents, four questions seem to come up over and over. They may be questions you have as well.

Question #1: How can I create a home committed to discipleship when no other parents seem to be doing it?

Any parent who strives to be intentional in the faith development of their kids might feel a bit countercultural. The reality is that few parents, even Christian ones, feel the burden of this need. You may feel alone. Your children, ever mindful of what everyone else is doing, may even think you're a bit strange. This tends to happen when values and practices at home aren't typical. But you can do two things to address this:

- *First, get used to it.* Jesus has called His disciples to an entirely different set of priorities than the world has. The more our culture moves away from God, the more you'll need to set a contrary standard in your home. Being radically different from the world is a fundamental reality your family can embrace and at times will need to endure. It won't always be easy.

- *Second, partner with others.* Ask God to bring other families with whom you can do life into your world. It may mean searching your church community for parents who already seem to be practicing intentional discipleship at home. Or it may mean sharing these principles with others with whom you're already in relationship in hopes they'll catch the vision as well.

We all need support and encouragement, especially when we endeavor to do hard things. The bottom line is that you'll likely be more successful if discipling in the home is lived out in community.

Question #2: What role does the church play in my children's faith development?

As we've said before, too many Christian parents depend on the church for all their kids' spiritual training and discipleship. Yet as we've also said, this is primarily a parent's job. But it sure is helpful when you feel like the church you attend supports your efforts. If you don't think your church is undergirding the spiritual training you're doing at home, your choices are limited: either find a new church or work to change the culture in your current one.

If you believe God is leading you to help your current church become more supportive of discipleship at home, move forward with wisdom. Church leadership can often feel defensive when church members suggest significant change. It can easily come off as criticism of what they're currently doing. Do all you can to work for change with an attitude of support. And if you want to see any new ministry at your church, volunteer to help create it. Most church leaders won't get excited about anything that adds to their already heavy workload.

Finally, don't underestimate the influence of the volunteer leaders who work with your kids. One thing the Fuller Youth Institute identified as key to the spiritual growth of teenagers is their having multiple adults besides their parents modeling and teaching a vibrant faith. They recommend a 5:1 adult-to-kid ratio, where parents aim to connect their teenagers to five adults who will pour into their kids' lives.[2] When you find adults like this at your church, see them as having a critical role in your children's discipleship journey.

Question #3: What if my kids are older and I'm starting too late? Is there any hope?

While the habits of discipleship are more easily established when your kids are young, they can still be developed when they're older. Rest assured that it's never too late to change course and commit yourself to what matters. It may be more challenging, but it can be done.

Maybe you need to start by simply calling a literal come-to-Jesus meeting—sitting your older children and teenagers down for a family discussion, sharing your convictions, and introducing some baby steps you want to try taking together. You don't need to have everything figured out. Just invite your kids into the discussion and ask them for ideas on what you might do as a family to become more active in knowing Jesus and following His ways.

Hopefully, if there's a solid commitment on your part and you don't give up when it gets challenging, your kids will see that discipleship is truly a part of your family's new normal.

Don't forget that Jesus' twelve disciples were already adults (some possibly teenagers) when He called them and started equipping them for kingdom living. After three years with Him—and a filling of the Holy Spirit—these men were able to change the world. This should remind you that influence is possible and that significant change in values and priorities can still be significant even when our kids are older. Again, it's never too late!

Question #4: What if my children reject the faith I'm trying to teach them?

While this discipleship paradigm is based on five key components in Jesus' model (and I believe it holds up biblically), you can't see them as a definitive checklist. As in, *If I do these five things, then these will be the guaranteed results.* No absolute guarantees regarding the fruit of your parenting efforts exist. There's the possibility that you'll prioritize each of the five things Jesus did with absolute excellence, but your kids still won't turn out like you hoped. If you recall, Judas was one of the Twelve, and he completely turned his back on Jesus. Your children might do likewise.

In that case, what else can you do, especially in this world where so many voices are vying for your kids' attention?

- Remember that the call remains for you to walk with God, follow Jesus' example, and live each day with intention.
- Remain committed to loving your kids unconditionally. Make sure they know and experience clear examples of your commitment to them.
- When you mess up, accept the extravagant grace of the cross and keep going.
- If your kids don't embrace Jesus, pray your guts out for them—without ceasing. God will never stop pursuing your children, so you can choose to never stop praying that they will stumble in such a way that He'll catch them when they fall.

No matter the outcome in both the short and long term, the command for parents to lead their kids to follow Jesus is absolutely nonnegotiable. Parents teaching children from one generation to the next is the primary model God established for the building up of His name, His people, and His kingdom.

This is beautifully characterized in Psalm 78:

> My people, hear my teaching;
>> listen to the words of my mouth.
> I will open my mouth with a parable;
>> I will utter hidden things, things from of old—

things we have heard and known,
  things our ancestors have told us.
We will not hide them from their descendants;
  we will tell the next generation
the praiseworthy deeds of the LORD,
  his power, and the wonders he has done.
He decreed statutes for Jacob
  and established the law in Israel,
which he commanded our ancestors
  to teach their children,
so the next generation would know them,
  even the children yet to be born,
  and they in turn would tell their children.
Then they would put their trust in God
  and would not forget his deeds
  but would keep his commands.

Psalm 78:1–7

Generational discipleship is God's powerful design. He doesn't necessarily need us, but He lovingly invites us to join Him in His work. What a privilege! You can choose to believe that God will honor your faithfulness even if things don't turn out in the exact way or timeframe you envision.

Take Spiritual Inventory

Before you take action and move forward, it might be helpful to form an accurate picture of where you are now. When I

Disciple Them like Jesus

presented our Discipling Home model in chapter 2, I invited you to give yourself a grade for each of the five components. If you did that, go back to pages 53–54 or to your notebook or journal and see what you recorded.

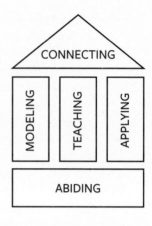

Then consider changes you might need to make, jotting down two or three action steps you believe God has stirred in you as you've worked through this book. You might have already recorded some of those action steps using the For Personal Reflection sections, but that's okay. Now you can record them all in one place.

1. Abiding: Walking with God

What was your grade?

What needs to change in you or in your home to grow in this area?

160

What are two or three specific action steps you can take?

2. Modeling: Living an Authentic Christian Life

What was your grade?

What needs to change in you or in your home to grow in this area?

What are two or three specific action steps you can take?

3. Teaching: Pointing Your Children to the Truth

What was your grade?

What needs to change in you or in your home to grow in this area?

What are two or three specific action steps you can take?

4. Applying: Giving Your Children Opportunities to Live Out Their Faith

What was your grade?

What needs to change in you or in your home to grow in this area?

What are two or three specific action steps you can take?

5. Connecting: Developing and Maintaining a Love Relationship with Your Children

What was your grade?

What needs to change in you or in your home to grow in this area?

What are two or three specific action steps you can take?

If you feel beat down or discouraged after evaluating your discipling role with your kids, take heart. God sees you and loves you just where you are. He wants to tenderly lead you to grow more intentional as a parent. Consider this truth found in Romans 8:1: "There is now no condemnation for those who are in Christ Jesus." If you're feeling condemned and discouraged, that's not from Jesus. He loves you and believes in you.

To be sure, I've failed more often than I succeeded in applying these parenting principles. Still, I'm confident that Jesus is faithful to fill in the missing places where I dropped the ball. That's the simple grace of God at work.

He wants to work in you as well. Simply start where you are and ask God to guide you to take whatever initial steps you need to take in each of the five discipling components modeled by Jesus.

Be the Extraordinary Parent Who Actually Does Something

It's easy to be convicted of a need for fundamental change regarding how you think, believe, or act. Yet too many people never follow through. They continue to be distracted by whatever "urgent" thing they think requires their immediate attention and never make the required adjustments to shift the rhythm of their lives.

Don't be that person. Don't be that parent.

The call to intentionally make disciples in the home is given to anyone God has entrusted with children. Most of the time that's a parent's role, but sometimes it falls to a grandparent or even a foster parent. No matter what, it's a solemn calling and your most important job. If God is with you—and He is—then you have what it takes to do this. No matter your upbringing, past failures, lack of training, or anything else the enemy might bring to mind to discourage you, you *can* lead the kids in your home to follow after Jesus.

To bring about lasting change in how you disciple your children, it would help to consider the three keys to making the paradigm shift I mentioned: how you think, believe, and act.

1. Change Your Thinking

The bulk of the content in this book is designed to educate, to get you to think differently about your role as a Christian parent. Hopefully, you've learned a few things. If you want to further process what all this means and what you'll do about it, talk it over with someone you trust: your spouse, a mentor, your Christian friends. Don't allow these ideas to go in one ear and out the other. Let them settle into your heart, and then ask God to change the way you see your role as a parent.

2. Believe You Can Do This

For a paradigm to truly shift in your home and to see lasting fruit in your kids, have confidence that you can become a discipling parent. In Christ, you have everything you need to be intentional in how you lead your children to follow Jesus. Gone are the days when you see taking your kids to church as your primary means of growing their faith. You can begin taking personal responsibility for their understanding of who God is and how they can find their place in His big story. You've got this!

3. Act Even If It's Awkward and Uncomfortable

Discipling your kids the way Jesus did with His twelve disciples might feel odd at first, especially if you've never done anything like it before. So this is a good time to remember what G. K. Chesterton said, as shared in chapter 5: "If a thing is worth doing, it is worth doing badly."

As with any new endeavor, like playing a sport or developing a skill, you have to be okay with being bad for a while if you're ever going to get good. While you're stumbling through new objectives and conversations and disciplines in your home, it's okay to ask your kids to be gracious while you're figuring it all out.

We all need grace in our families. Mountains and mountains of grace. We need it from our kids as we awkwardly try to teach them to love Jesus. We need it from our spouses when we let them down. And we need it from God as we stumble through our imperfect and normal family lives. For we are all fallen moms and dads who want to do right but more often than not come up way too short.

Thankfully, grace is one thing our extravagant God generously offers us daily. It's the root of our salvation ("While we were still sinners, Christ died for us"—Romans 5:8), and it covers our every failure ("Where sin increased, grace increased all the more"—Romans 5:20).

The good news for our parenting life is that Christ fills in every gap where we feel inadequate. Paul shares what God told him about his own shortcomings in 2 Corinthians 12:9: "My grace is sufficient for you, for my power is made perfect in weakness." If you feel ill-prepared in this area of parenting, there's good news: God has made room to become incredibly big and influential in that part of your life—if only you'll let Him.

So that's my invitation at the end of this story, for you to ask God to do a big work of grace in your parenting. For you to ask Him to show up in supernatural ways you can't explain. For you to see Him at work in your home because you take a few baby steps of obedience. For you to shift your family's focus away from the American Dream and toward the building of God's kingdom.

Imagine it happening, because it absolutely can. God willed for these things to be true in your home before He even created the world. He's looking for moms and dads willing to lay down their own agendas and join Him in His plan to make disciples of all people—starting with their own children.

So what are you waiting for?

Epilogue

Thoughts on Children and Salvation

Where does a child's salvation fit into the parents' desire to intentionally disciple their kids?

This book has a lot to say about discipleship but not much to say about a child's salvation. This is because the Gospels have a lot to say about our being a disciple of Jesus but not so much about how today's evangelical Christians view salvation.

Yes, I believe in the need to be "born again." My evangelical upbringing and John 3 have driven into me the importance of that moment when a person decides to follow Jesus. In every Christian's life should be a clear understanding of the moment they repented of their sin, placed their faith in Jesus, and moved from death to life in Christ. The New Testament documents the moment many people chose to place their faith in Him.

But Jesus mainly called people to follow Him, and this happened in a variety of ways. The original disciples were invited to lay down their fishing nets and become fishers of men, and they did. The thief on the cross trusted Jesus moments before he died. And both adults and children chose to respond to the apostles' invitation to follow the ways of Christ throughout the book of Acts. They found new life in Jesus in all shapes and sizes, but what each of them had in common was their choice to change the direction of their life and to start following Him.

Note that Jesus' Great Commission in Matthew 28:18–20 commands us to "make disciples," not converts. The call is to teach people to obey everything Jesus commanded, not to walk an aisle or say a prayer.

But what about children specifically?

Different Branches of Christianity Disagree on How a Child Comes to Faith

Evangelicals might say children, like adults, "make a decision to follow Jesus." Reformed believers might suggest that children are "born into the covenant." And Catholic believers perform a christening on their infants and then have a young adolescent go through a confirmation of their faith. So there's great diversity within the body of Christ, the millions of brothers and sisters who trust in Jesus' work on the cross alone for their salvation.

So though we might disagree theologically on how and when a child can come to faith, anyone who has even a basic knowledge of the New Testament would agree with the fundamental call to be a disciple. And I want to make an argument that, scripturally, following Jesus is more important than how you get there.

Salvation Is to Discipleship What a Wedding Is to Marriage

There's simply so much more in the Bible about what it means to be a disciple of Jesus than about the moment of salvation that began your relationship with Him. And the dynamics of this might be compared to marriage, a metaphor frequently used in the New Testament to describe our relationship to God.

If you ask me if I'm married, I probably won't pull out wedding photos or a marriage license a minister filed with the state to prove I am. No, I'll introduce you to my wife: "Here's the person I share a life and home with. She's the woman, right here in the flesh, to whom I've been married for the majority of my life."

What's important is not what happened to me three long decades ago. Instead, what matters most is my reality today: I'm married. In the same way, too many times, when asked about their grown child's faith (particularly a child who's "walked away" from it), parents cling to a decision their son or daughter made when they were young and reason that their salvation is surely secure.

They tend to ignore the fact that there's no evidence of any life change when comparing the before and after of that moment. They forget the fact that the child has now chosen a worldview, values, and priorities that don't include God and His kingdom in any shape or form. They reason that their child *must* be a Christian because of that decision they made when they were young.

For parents who see their young adult children living far from God, this can be a reasonable attempt to placate their dissonant and grieving souls. They can desperately cling to a decision their child made when they were younger to give them hope for their eternal condition. I get it. Still, I just don't think we can call someone a Christian if they're not at some level striving to follow Jesus in the here and now.

Unbiblical Language to Describe Christian Discipleship

In modern Christianity, we've become comfortable with far too many terms and phrases not found in the Bible, resulting in an unbiblical understanding of Christian discipleship. They're confusing and ultimately result in poor theology. Here are three that come to mind:

"Pray the sinner's prayer."

There's no sinner's prayer in the Bible, and we (particularly evangelicals) have placed far too much emphasis on the idea.

We've treated it almost as a special code one must recite to secure their eternity in heaven. This has led so many people to believe they're a Christian because of the prayer they prayed when they were a child. But remember, Jesus calls people to follow Him, not to pray a certain prayer.

Consider a better option. As you lead your children to embrace the faith, talk about the fact that their sin separates them from God and that they're desperately in need of His forgiveness. Discuss what it means to count the cost of following Jesus (it could even cost them their lives). If they recognize the brokenness of their sin and their need for salvation, lead them to call out to God in faith and repentance.

This may require time to process, and their prayer should be personal. Sure, you can guide them, but don't settle for a repeat-after-me prayer that lacks real, personal substance and conviction. And if your child is too young to do that by themselves, I argue that they're too young to grasp what they're doing.

"Ask Jesus Christ into your heart."

I think this language breeds confusion, especially for children. *Asking Jesus into your heart* is an abstract concept, and kids' thinking is concrete. They can't comprehend what we mean when we say it, and I believe we should tenaciously work to remove this phrase from our churches.

I know it might seem heretical to suggest that Billy Graham got something wrong, but our greatest modern evangelist used to say, "There is a hole in our heart that only God can fill."[1] I disagree. The truth is your entire life is a God-shaped void. It's not that everything else is there and He's the final puzzle piece that brings it all together once He "comes into your heart." Your very existence is meaningless apart from Jesus. He desires to fill up absolutely everything you are with Himself, His ways, and His calling on your life.

"When I was a child, I made Jesus my Savior; when I was older, I made Him my Lord."

I honestly roll my eyes when I hear someone say this when sharing their Christian testimony. It's not biblical, and it's not how we become Christ-followers. When Jesus called His disciples (and when the early apostles called people to follow Jesus), it was a leave-everything-behind-and-be-all-in call. This isn't a two-step process that takes years to develop. It's a false faith rooted in nothing of real substance.

It's far from the biblical discipleship Jesus calls people to. A.W. Tozer described this heresy as "the widely accepted concept that we humans can choose to accept Christ only because we need Him as Savior and that we have the right to postpone our obedience to Him as Lord as long as we want to!"[2]

Every person's story is unique, and as they grow, they ideally give Christ more and more control of their life. But if someone truly ascribes to the two-stage "Savior, then Lord" process of faith, I suggest that the time they chose to make

Jesus Lord was when they were born again. Everything before that was superficial lip service.

So What's a Parent to Do?

Consider taking these steps:

First and foremost, if you're in an evangelical tradition, stop living in fear about "getting your child saved." Too many parents lose sleep over the fact that their eight-year-old hasn't yet made a decision to follow Jesus. While this is certainly at the top of your parental priorities, you can choose to stop living in fear that your child could go to hell.

We don't believe in a God who sends children to hell, particularly those who don't have the capacity for abstract thought (under thirteen or fourteen). Many of the principles found in Scripture and basic atonement theology are abstract in nature, and I simply cannot accept that God would hold a child accountable for what they can't fully understand. But we can teach biblical truths and the ways of Jesus to our kids and see it as laying the foundation for when they can make a decision of their will to follow Him with their lives.

In three decades of pastoral work, I've just heard too many stories about young children coming to Christ, being baptized, and then encountering God in their teen years and admitting that they didn't have a clue what they were doing back then. (In fact, I think the baptism numbers in large evangelical denominations are hugely overblown because so many of our kids have been baptized twice.)

Encourage your child to wait a little longer to make a profession of faith. In a wine commercial aired from 1978 to 1981, actor Orson Welles would quote Paul Masson and say, "We will sell no wine before its time." In that same vein, I would argue that "you can't get a child saved until you get them lost."

There's a huge difference between a child's understanding of their sin and a teenager's. We can tell a child she needs Jesus because she's done bad things, but it takes convincing. On the other hand, a teenager can better grasp the depravity of her heart, her rebellion against God, and her desperate need for a Savior. When these young adolescents legitimately cry out to Jesus, it's more likely to be real and life-changing.

When I was on a mission trip serving in a thriving church in Norway, I witnessed the baptism of eighteen-to-twenty-year-olds. I asked a sixteen-year-old, "Have you been baptized yet?" His response? "I'm not ready." In their tradition, you couldn't fully commit until you had some time to live life and fully "consider the cost." I'm convinced that our young children can't do that. I'm not suggesting that the practice of this Scandinavian church become the norm for everyone, but it's food for thought.

Even if you think your child has trusted Christ and is following Him as best they can as His disciple, you may want them to hold off on public baptism a little longer. This is only because childhood memories can become blurry over time, and you want baptism to be a clear memory and marker of their decision to follow Christ.

Celebrate each step in your child's spiritual journey. As you disciple them, your kids will no doubt experience amazing markers of spiritual growth. Celebrate them. Anytime you see them having an aha moment about their need for Jesus and the part they play in God's kingdom, affirm them. Make a big deal out of each time they take a step toward Christ.

Finally, before your child makes a decision of their will to surrender their life to God, you can begin to disciple them by:

- Prioritizing your own relationship with God, striving to walk daily in the Spirit's power, abiding in Christ.
- Modeling and teaching the ways of Jesus in everyday life in your home and world.
- Fueling every opportunity for your child to experience God. In the life you lead and in the daily practice of your home, give them chances to apply what they learn so they can "taste and see that the LORD is good" (Psalm 34:8).

Hopefully, through all this your kids will long to follow God and make His priorities their priorities. And you can do it all in the context of the love relationship you have with them. As long as you stay close to God and listen to His voice, you'll always have exactly what you need to foster the discipling home God has called you to establish. Never forget that.

Acknowledgments

To my wife, Jenifer—you've followed me into all the hard places ministry has taken us and put up with me for three and a half decades. I thank you more than I can say. And to my children—thank you for giving me immeasurable grace for those times I didn't fully live out the truths found within these pages. God is ever faithful even when your dad is imperfect and falls short.

To the many people who helped me edit and refine these words—Teena, Amy, Rob, Lee, Kristi, Stephen, David, Adrian, Jennifer, Teisha, Stephen, Sally, and others who read early drafts—thank you! You helped make this work better. Editor Jean Bloom used her gifts to make my words clearer, and Andy McGuire and the team at Bethany House have made the entire publishing process a joy.

I also need to give a big shout-out to Dr. Rick Yount, my favorite seminary professor from back in the day. He showed me how a simple model drawn on a napkin can clarify some of the fundamental purposes of our lives.

Many thanks to all the people who have been impacted by the work of I.N.F.O. for Families over the past decade. You have listened to us speak, read our words, liked our posts on social media, and even supported our ministry. We do what we do because of imperfect and normal families like yours and ours.

Beyond all this, my greatest thanks go to my heavenly Father. Every good and perfect gift in my life has come from You. Thank You for allowing me to be the steward of this message. May every parent who reads these words disciple their kids a little bit more like Jesus did.

Discipleship Resources for the Home

Family Time Training: FamTime.com

Expository Parenting Ministries: ExpositoryParenting.org

Connected Families: ConnectedFamilies.org

Visionary Family Ministries: VisionaryFam.com

D6: D6Family.com

The National Center for Biblical Parenting: BiblicalParenting.org

The INFO for Families app: Subsplash.com/InfoForFamilies/app

Notes

Chapter 1 Parenting's Primary Purpose

1. Ron Burgundy in the film *Anchorman: The Legend of Rob Burgundy*, directed by Adam McKay, written by Will Ferrell and Adam McKay, Dreamworks Pictures, 2004.

2. Bunmi Laditan, May 1, 2017, Facebook, https://www.facebook.com/BunmiK Laditan/photos/a.1397535887160070/1899244270322560?type=3.

3. Steve Farrar, as overheard at The Men's Conference at Johnson Ferry Baptist Church, Marietta, Georgia, March 15, 2008.

Chapter 2 Disciple like Jesus

1. J. Loren Norris, "Live a More Excellent Life," Online Seminar, https://www.jlorennorris.com/store/p5/Live-a-more-excellent-life-online-course.html.

Chapter 3 Abiding: Walking with God

1. Henry T. Blackaby and Richard Blackaby, *Experiencing God Day By Day Devotional* (Nashville: B&H Publishing Group, 2006), 337.

2. Bruce Wilkinson with David Kopp, *Secrets of the Vine: Breaking Through to Abundance* (Colorado Springs: Multnomah Books, 2012), 96.

3. Wilkinson, *Secrets of the Vine*, 97.

4. Brother Lawrence, *The Practice of the Presence of God* (New Delhi: Delhi Open Books, 2020), Kindle edition.

Chapter 4 Modeling: Living an Authentic Christian Life

1. Phillips, Craig & Dean, "I Want to Be Just Like You," *Lifeline,* Star Song, 1994, https://www.azlyrics.com/lyrics/phillipscraigdean/iwanttobejustlikeyou.html.

2. Kevin DeYoung, "Reaching the Next Generation: Hold Them With Holiness," The Gospel Coalition, U.S. Edition, October 21, 2009, https://www.thegospelcoalition.org/blogs/kevin-deyoung/reaching-the-next-generation-hold-them-with-holiness/.

3. U2, "I Still Haven't Found What I'm Looking For," by Paul David Hewson, Adam Clayton, Larry Mullen, and Dave Evans, produced by Daniel Lanois and Brian Eno, track 2 on *The Joshua Tree,* Island Records, 1987.

4. George Barna, quoted in "Christian Parents' 'Scrambled Philosophy of Life' Turns Children Away from Christianity: Barna," by Ryan Foley, *The Christian Post,* April 14, 2022, https://www.christianpost.com/news/barna-christian-parents-scrambled-worldview-harms-kids-faith.html.

5. Kevin Huggins and Phil Landrum, *Guiding Your Teen to a Faith That Lasts* (Grand Rapids, MI: Discovery House Publishers, 1994), 23–25.

6. Huggins and Landrum, *Guiding Your Teen to a Faith That Lasts,* 25–27.

Chapter 5 Teaching: Pointing Your Children to the Truth

1. Charles Haddon Spurgeon, "The Sunday-School and the Scriptures," The Spurgeon Center, October 18, 1885, https://www.spurgeon.org/resource-library/sermons/the-sunday-school-and-the-scriptures/#flipbook/.

2. "Parents Baffled That 1 Hour Of Youth Group A Week Not Effectively Combating Teen's 30 Hours On TikTok," *The Babylon Bee,* March 17, 2022, https://babylonbee.com/news/parents-baffled-that-1-hour-of-youth-group-a-week-not-effectively-combating-teens-30-hours-on-tiktok.

3. Gilbert Keith Chesterton, *What's Wrong with the World* (New York: Dodd, Mead and Company, 1910), 320.

Chapter 6 Applying: Giving Your Children Opportunities to Live Out Their Faith

1. Neil McClendon, as spoken from the stage at various ministry student ministry events, 1995 to present.

2. Christian Smith with Melinda Lundquist Denton, *Soul Searching: The Religious and Spiritual Lives of American Teenagers* (New York: Oxford University Press, 2005), 163.

3. Ann Kovalchick and Kara Dawson, Eds., *Education and Technology: An Encyclopedia* (Santa Barbara: ABC-CLIO, 2004), 161.

4. Valerie Strauss, "Why the 'Learning Pyramid' Is Wrong," *The Washington Post*, March 6, 2013, https://www.washingtonpost.com/news/answer-sheet/wp/2013/03/06/why-the-learning-pyramid-is-wrong/.

Chapter 7 Connecting: Developing and Maintaining a Love Relationship with Your Children

1. Jill Briscoe, Pastor's Retreat at The Cove, May 19, 2011.

2. Gary Chapman, *The 5 Love Languages: How to Express Heartfelt Commitment to Your Mate*, reprint edition (Oregon City, OR: Northfield Publishing, 2015).

3. Robert L. Leahy PhD, "How Big a Problem Is Anxiety?" *Psychology Today*, April 30, 2008, https://www.psychologytoday.com/us/blog/anxiety-files/200804/how-big-problem-is-anxiety.

4. From Chris Liebrum, used with permission.

Chapter 8 Now Go Make Disciples

1. Francis Chan with Mark Beuving, *Multiply: Disciples Making Disciples* (Colorado Springs, CO: David C Cook, 2012), 31.

2. Dr. Kara E. Powell and Dr. Chap Clark, *Sticky Faith: Everyday Ideas to Build Lasting Faith in Your Kids* (Grand Rapids: Zondervan, 2011), 101.

Epilogue Thoughts on Children and Salvation

1. Billy Graham, "Can Revival Come?" *Southern Equip*, October 16, 2014, https://equip.sbts.edu/article/can-revival-come/.

2. A.W. Tozer, *I Call It Heresy* (Camp Hill: Zur Ltd., 1991), 1.

Barrett Johnson

founded I.N.F.O. for Families in 2014 to help "Imperfect & Normal Families Only" stay informed, equipped, and on task. A popular communicator and writer on marriage and family life, he is committed to encouraging parents as they help their kids navigate our hypersexualized and technologically driven culture. His favorite job is speaking to church, school, and community groups about the challenges of modern parenting.

Barrett spent twenty-five years ministering to students and families through the local church, most recently serving as the Minister to Families at Johnson Ferry Baptist Church outside Atlanta, Georgia. He and his wife, Jenifer, are native Texans who currently live in Atlanta. They have five children and seven grandchildren.

Connect with Barrett:

INFOForFamilies.com

Facebook @INFOForFamilies

Instagram @BarrettJohnsonInfo

TikTok @InfoForFamilies

X @InfoForFamilies

Subsplash.com/InfoForFamilies/app